I0472160

PLAY

With Blocks, Chess, and Monopoly at Work

ERIK N. BOE

To all who go to work every day to make the world a better place.

CONTENTS

1

Introduction

Thank you for reading this book! Should you decide to complete it, it will be worth the effort. This book will provide you a useful, unique, and fun way of looking at the dynamics of everyday work events. In a few hours, you will gain insight into what has taken me a lifetime to learn and validate. In my case, a "lifetime" is five thousand working days.

I started out exploring a career through safe routes like books, schools, odd jobs, and internships. I studied management, economics, and international business. But most of all I explored computer science, the then-rising star of the technology universe. I learned to speak several languages, such as French and English. Finally, I was ready for my first real job. I found the perfect one at Apple, in the international software group, testing the German and French versions of the Macintosh operating system. I soon took on a leadership role in the group. The job had everything I was looking for—international high tech in corporate America.

It was a dream job, so I put everything I had into it. I spent endless hours learning and looking for ways of making an impact. I wanted to apply the many things I had learned while preparing for my first real job. I soon found an opportunity to improve things, and I proposed a project to my immediate managers. They agreed to let me try it. Thus, my journey of learning about work dynamics started.

The project was a big failure. I did everything right, but nothing came of it. I was trying to change how Apple developed and delivered its international software, which at that time was done one language version after another—sometimes more than one year later. Every time a new version of the operating systems was developed, it was translated (or localized) and released one at a time. Some languages, such as French, could be localized, documented and tested within months. Others, such as Japanese, would take much longer because of the many technical challenges around the large character set. It was clear to me and many others that including all languages in the one release was the way of the future. Fast forward. That future is here today. Just look at your iPhone and see how easy it is to change language settings. With just a few clicks you can move from one language to another. But that was not the norm when I proposed my project.

My project did not result in releasing all languages at once. In fact, nothing changed. None of the benefits, such as reduced development costs, improved product quality, faster time to market, and improved customer satisfaction was realized.

After this failure, I started to investigate what had gone wrong by asking myself questions. How had seemingly reasonable steps led me in the wrong direction? What factors make a project successful? What leads to failure?

I dug deeper. I wanted to understand patterns that lead to failure or success. Since I spent so much time in meetings that seemed to be good place to start. What would happen when an executive attended a meeting? Would he or she influence key decisions? What would happen when a group of peers met? Who would then be able to influence the direction of the meeting? Did people honor commitments that were made in meetings? If not, why? Why would projects run by John be successful, but Paul's would repeatedly fail? Why would Susan always get the largest part of the budget?

Why did my project fail? It took me a year to understand that it was not a failure of reason or effort, but rather one of ignorance about forces that are present at work. I slowly started to see things differently. What were once dark mysteries became familiar stories. Invisible light transformed into a rainbow of colors. An incomprehensible dynamic seen through these new lenses revealed blueprints with hidden messages. What I had not been taught in business school became a series of patterns assembled right in front of my eyes. This discovery led me to new and amazing insights.

By the way, my project failed because of many shortcomings. Here are a few: Lack of executive support; I did not spend enough time to understand the different motivations across all impacted groups; the benefits were not well articulated; I did not ensure that all teams had the ability to absorb changes in priorities; and finally, I did not define a solution that was implementable in bite-sized changes. I will stop here.

How does clarity emerge? Is it just the passing of time? Are colleagues slowly revealing pieces of the puzzle until it is complete? Is it like bird-watching, where you quietly walk around in the forest and jot down detailed notes? Or are you and your friends sharing insights until all is clear? It might be all of the above, but at its core the answer is pattern recognition. By observing similar events playing out over and over, you start to anticipate outcomes. You envision results down to the biggest smile, the loudest cry, or something in between.

But in order to attain clarity, you have to look for patterns, reasons why events unfold in certain ways. Pattern recognition demands focus and dedication combined with constantly asking why. As humans, emotions and desires often steer us to abandon logic. It can be difficult to apply logic if we are heavily invested in the outcome of a particular situation. It is very tempting to make everything at work personal. If you take this road, patterns do not emerge as easily. Instead, you collect reasons why everybody else is wrong. There are choices to be had, and the big one is either to build a world around you that supports your own beliefs or to scrutinize your view of the world in order to gain clarity. Are you willing to spend the effort finding underlying patterns that can help you decipher the world? If so, know that it takes time to peel out initial observations in order to discern them.

Pattern recognition is not the same as validating a point of view. If you put on blue glasses, everything will look blue to you. If you always look for the bad side of people, then you tend to overlook the good side. Pattern recognition is not a worldview or an attitude. Rather, it is observing something and comparing it to something else. If you find a match or a near match, then you may be able to use that information to make better decisions. But forcing a match will not help you. Pretending everything is the same is to put on blinders, and that will render you ignorant of the situation at hand. Instead, you have to be open to finding the right match, the right pattern.

Why do patterns matter? What if you find one? How can you use this insight? The short answer is that it will help you make better decisions. A situation that resembles another may have similar probabilities with regard to outcomes. In other words, it will help you understand what is likely to occur next. This leads to better decisions, and better decisions will make you more successful. It all starts with patterns and pattern recognition.

This book reveals patterns I have discovered and validated through firsthand experiences during my life in corporate America. I will now share these patterns with you to dramatically increase your chances of success.

2

Forces at Work

Do you dread waking up and going to work because you feel like you are wasting your life? Do you feel stuck? Do less talented people around you get promoted? Are people at work focused on themselves rather than company success? Do you see yourself as if you were in an ant colony preparing for rain, always scurrying around? Are you like a worker ant carrying more supplies than you should for little or no recognition? If this is how you feel, it is time for a change that starts now.

But first, let me ask: should work be easy? Should everything fall into your lap? That would be great, but the world is wired differently than that. Just like in the ant colony, success requires effort. By definition, work means applying mental or physical effort in order to achieve results. So no, work is not meant to be easy. But is work meant to be fun? Is work meant to be rewarding? Let's explore that further.

Make Work Rewarding

It is time to look at work in a different way that will help you achieve success. It will not make work easier, but it will make it more fun and rewarding. It certainly has for me. Nothing absolves you from doing your job well and fulfilling your role. After all, that is what you are paid for.

Doing your best every day is a prerequisite for success. Throwing in the towel is not a path toward greatness. This is not a book about showing you shortcuts or relying on luck. You cannot be successful if everything you do is linked to poor performance or chaos, so your only option is to do your job the best it possibly can be done, regardless of your current circumstances. That is the baseline from which you can take on new challenges.

Success is about understanding the world around you, learning new skills, and then applying this newfound knowledge to create your own outcomes. As with everything new, it will take some time to understand and put into practice. That aside, you will now learn new skills that will require additional effort in these areas.

1. Decide to excel in your current role, starting today.
2. Learn success skills by spending a few days reading this book.
3. Implement new skills during the next three to six months.
4. Continue to refine your skills.

With these in mind, let's take a look at what is happening at work every day in every company in every country in the world. Everywhere? Yes, what is happening at work today has been occurring for thousands of years. It is something that is a result of being human and part of a society that organizes into groups to achieve specific goals. A company is a recent construct that reveals dynamics linked to these facts.

Forces at Work

"May the force be with you." This statement is part of every *Star Wars* movie ever made. The intent is to support the hero in his or her battles against evil in the universe. And in these movies, it works! So clearly, a universal force is out there for those who are worthy and can find a way to tap into its powers.

Forces are also found here on planet earth. In fact, they show up for work every day, everywhere. Sometimes they help you, sometimes not. You may not see them, but you can feel their presence. You know that something is happening, but you may not be able to put your finger on it. You may scratch your head and wonder how this particular outcome came to be. Nothing could have predicted it.

Let's look at some typical situations where forces are influencing what is happening at work.

The promotion: The best programmer and engineer is promoted into management. This often happens in high-tech or creative organizations where the value of management is low and managers are expected to be working managers (building products and solutions in addition to managing teams). Unfortunately, if the new manager ends up being your manager, your job is now turned into a competition. Your manager is constantly showing you that he or she still has it. In the process, your boss forgets to manage the team, and you suffer.

The desperate team: Your development team is frustrated that product management is constantly changing priorities. You can't understand why making decisions is so difficult. Nothing gets done. No success is in sight. Before long, the whole team is doing nothing but complaining about everything. How did it come to this?

The troubled employee: An employee who is unable to find the right team reaches out to executives to ask them to fix his problems. They offer support and decide to move the employee into a new role. But after a while, the problem-employee returns to them, saying he still feels that nothing has changed. According to him, the executives do not know how to run the company. What is going on here?

The new product idea: You have a great idea for a new product. You have boundless insight into how to obtain significant market share. You create an excellent presentation that is bulletproof and rehearse it until it becomes a work of art. But less than three minutes into the presentation, the executives shut down your proposal. What went wrong?

The project cancellation: You walk into the office and find out that your project is canceled. The day before, everything was just fine. In fact, it was a model project. Everyone agreed that it was how a project should be run. What happened?

The resource ask: You do a presentation for senior management, but do not make it beyond the first slide. You wanted to ask for additional resources for your project, but instead you leave the meeting with more problems and action items that can fill the next three months. How did that happen?

The annual reorganization: Your group has finally figured out how to get things done in an efficient manner. Then, all of a sudden, there is a reorganization. All the groups around you change names, and different leaders are appointed. Now you have to spend the next three months rebuilding your network and deciphering the best ways of getting things accomplished. Why?

The new company-wide initiative: Executives brought in a consulting company to fix the slow-moving development process, and your project has been selected as the first one to be scrutinized—or, should I say, to benefit from these new ideas. You now have to spend the next three months hoping to survive the scrutiny. What is the best strategy, join or avoid?

The lack of executive support: Nothing seems to get done. It is impossible to stay focused on anything long enough to prove that it will work or not. As a result, your team is seeking a sponsor high up in the organization to help them remove roadblocks. They are looking for executive support through decisions in their favor or to have their back. But despite high hopes, nothing changes. In fact, the hope that the sponsor would make your life easier is shattered. What is wrong with your executives?

These nine scenarios occur quite frequently. What do they have in common? First, they may seem somewhat arbitrary or illogical. And second, some of them probably already have happened to you. If so, why? Why can't you avoid these situations altogether?

You may not be able to avoid them. That is like using a "Get Out of Jail Free" card whenever something happens that you don't like. The main challenge is that the forces behind these events seem invisible. Most likely, every one of these situations will happen again and again. You may not know exactly when, or what or whom it will involve, but you can decrease the possibilities of these situations occurring in the first place and be prepared by having a countermove ready. But before diving into the details, let's name and define the forces at play.

Dynamics

This book is about understanding work dynamics so you can become successful in your current and future roles. You can also use these insights to design and run a successful organization. If you already manage a company, you can use this book to redesign and improve how your company works to deliver better results.

I will focus on three categories of the many dynamics that are at play in an organization. I have focused on these three because they are pervasive and have great impact on a company. They are not readily visible or easily understood. They are neither typically discussed nor are they covered as part of official company communication, but they are real. Your success hinges upon understanding and mastering these dynamics. You can ignore them and become successful, but only with a lot of luck. This book will reveal how these powerful dynamics work so that luck is not your default path to success.

First, you have to understand what these dynamics are and where they are. In every company there are many variations of these dynamics at play. Different events will influence dynamics in subtle ways. Each and every company is unique and faces different challenges. But all their employees are entangled with the same core set of rules. Understanding these rules will help you develop a winning strategy. But before we get into the dynamics and the rules, let's look at some fun toys and games that have been around for a while.

3

The Games

Dynamics are not described by their shape or size, but rather by their rules and their current state. I will refer to these dynamics as games. I do this because dynamics are just like games. The world looks chaotic when you don't know what game is being played and what rules are in place, as there are no discernible patterns to help you decipher it.

If you look at a game you have not seen before, it may be difficult to recognize the rules. Even worse, it will be extremely frustrating to play without knowing the rules or having had time to practice. But if you play long enough and ask other players for hints, you can learn the rules and may eventually master the game.

Most games are designed to last a relatively short period of time, allowing a player to learn and improve rather quickly. This approach works well when the game has a name and a written set of rules that fits neatly inside the box in which the game is packaged. At work, it is a little more challenging to learn the rules, so let's start with these simpler games.

There are three universal invisible forces—or dynamics—taking place in every organization. They can be best described as blocks, chess, and Monopoly. Before diving into how they play out in organizations, let's look at these games and toys as they were originally designed.

Blocks

There are many types of toy blocks and bricks that encourage creativity. Lincoln Logs was invented by John Lloyd Wright around 1916. John was the son of famed architect Frank Lloyd Wright. The first notched miniature set of logs were based upon the Imperial Hotel in Tokyo, designed by John's father. Since then, more than one hundred million sets have been sold worldwide. In 1999, Lincoln Logs entered The National Toy Hall of Fame, and today is still a very popular toy.

Another modular toy is trains on wooden tracks. It is a simple toy that allows for building your own personal railroad. Production of these toys started in the United States in 1936. In 1957, BRIO from Sweden introduced the peg and hole system to connect the tracks. It made it simpler to build a track. The magnets on the end of the trains made connecting the trains a breeze. This simplicity made this type of toy broadly appealing. Every boy I know at some point has owned wooden tracks and toy trains, including my own son.

Growing up, my favorite pastime was to play with LEGO bricks. They are interlocking, plastic, and standardized components that lets you build almost anything you can imagine. Before being released to market, the bricks are tested for durability: chemical, mechanical, electrical, flammability safety, and hygiene. The quality of LEGO bricks is tremendous. I still have some that look the same as when I was a young boy. People who buy them are very likely to recommend them to others. They provide an experience that almost anyone can relate to.

The LEGO Group, which was founded in Denmark in 1932, has grown to become one of the largest toy companies in the world. The word "lego" was originally taken from a Danish phrase meaning, "Play well." LEGO started out with simple pieces. Through the years more and more special sets have been designed, such as complicated *Star Trek* spaceships with thousands of unique pieces. In the United States alone, more than a hundred new sets are introduced every year.

A basic LEGO brick is a two-by-four or eight-studded brick. According to the movie *A LEGO Brickumentary*, two eight-studded bricks can be combined in twenty-four different ways. Three eight-studded bricks can be combined in 1,060 ways. How many ways can six of them be combined? More than 915 million ways. Imagine you have a few hundred pieces. The number of combinations is almost limitless. LEGO bricks encourage creativity. It is enormously rewarding to see your ideas materialize in front of your own eyes, built by your own hands. Playing with LEGO bricks is really about setting your imagination free and having fun.

Chess

Played for more than fifteen hundred years, chess is a game of strategic skill for two players. Each player moves sixteen pieces across an eight-by-eight checkerboard according to a set of rules. The challenge is to predict and block your opponent's moves while trying to capture the opponent's king, which is called "checkmate."

Achieving checkmate requires multiple, carefully thought-out moves. This is mental gymnastics: to win, you must envision what will happen after four, five, or even six moves by both players.

There are a total of thirty-two pieces on the board at the start of a chess game. There are six types of pieces: pawns, knights, bishops, rooks, the queen, and the king. Each piece moves in a different way. Each player has one king, one queen, two knights, two bishops, two rooks, and eight pawns. There are more than nine million different possible positions after just three moves by each player, or a total of six moves. There are more than 288 billion different possible positions after four moves by each player, or eight moves. The number of forty-move games is bigger than the number of electrons in the known universe. That number is 10^{80}, also called the Eddington number. In other words, the game of chess may look simple, but the possible outcomes are almost endless.

It is estimated that 650 million people play chess today, a steady increase during the last fifty years. According to Wikipedia, since 1950, the chess community has designated about fifteen hundred grand masters, who are expert players and have scored extremely high in international competitions. It has been said that chess is a game that makes you think that the winner is a very intelligent person—and if you win, you think that *you* are a very intelligent person.

Monopoly

Monopoly was invented in the Unites States in 1903 and started being commercially sold in the 1930s. The game—whose board contains spaces named after properties in Atlantic City, New Jersey—has become part of popular world culture: it is sold in more than one hundred countries and has been translated into thirty-seven languages. This is according to Wikipedia and several other online sites.

In Monopoly, players engage in financial dealings using imitation money. The board has a total of forty spaces and twenty-eight properties: twenty-two streets that are designated by color, four railroads, and two utility spaces. There are also three spaces called Chance, three that are called Community Chest, a Luxury Tax space, and an Income Tax space. The four corners are named Go, Jail/Just Visiting, Free Parking, and Go to Jail. The game comes with thirty-two houses and twelve hotels, twenty-eight title deed cards, sixteen Chance cards, and sixteen Community Chest cards. The game used to contain a bank that totaled $15,140 in Monopoly money.

Monopoly is about winning at all costs by crushing opponents and leveraging power, money, and probability. The goal is to drive other players into bankruptcy, leaving one monopolist in control of the entire economy. The winning strategy is to build an inventory of money, properties, and other entities that provide regular revenue.

Based upon the rules and the fact the game uses two dice, it is possible to calculate the probabilities of landing on the various spaces. This can be used to help create a winning approach. Monopoly is not a game of luck;

rather, it is about incorporating probabilities into decision-making and understanding the rules and risks.

Now, let's take a look at the players of these games and toys—but in the workplace.

Erik N. Boe

4

The Players

So, who are playing with these toys and games? Take a look around your organization and ask yourself these three questions.

- Who likes to create and build things?
- Who is constantly planning and plotting to get ahead?
- Who are the risk-takers focused on winning at all costs?

This is not about a particular person, but rather about groups and collections of groups in a company. Collectively, their roles and attitudes can be placed into three categories. This is not to say that these are the only categories, but they are the most dominant and pervasive. They are found in every industry and company. These behaviors emerge as a result of humans being placed into groups that are guided by company goals, coupled with individual desire for success. Who are these people? How do they see the world around themselves? What do they like and dislike? Well, they are teams, management and executives.

Block Players

Developers, designers, engineers, and writers love to be creative. Product development teams love to build. They are always looking for problems to solve. They want to be creative, have fun, and change the world. For them, the world is filled with endless possibilities. They tend to avoid uncertainties and constant change. They simply want to be left alone with their team to do their work. They become irritated when they can't get the support they need to do their job.

Left alone, block or brick players will forever improve upon their original creation. The most prized skill in this group is envisioning a creation and dazzling everyone once it is completed. They do not like to spend time planning and reporting on progress. The process word is a bothersome thing that gets in their way of innovation. Managing people is not important; there is no creativity in that. It is a waste of time dealing with different groups and ideas. The only opinion that really matters is their own.

They are uncomfortable competing with other groups for resources. They avoid what they call political games, as they see them as a waste of time that lead to nothing but frustration. They want to build great products. They often say things like, "Just tell me what to do," "Make up your mind," and "Stop changing the plans!" For them, the world is simple. It can be summarized in one sentence: "Give me blocks or bricks, and get out of my way!"

Building with blocks or bricks is normally done by teams. They get together and agree on who will work on what part. The closer they work together, the faster and better the outcome is. However, some individuals prefer to work on their own to ensure their creativity is made visible for all to see. Playing with blocks is very different from the other two games where players are mostly individuals fending for themselves and their groups.

Chess Players

Middle management is always looking to acquire more resources and better technologies. They are constantly competing with other groups for a pool of resources. In this game, they can show how smart they are by predicting what others will do and how to best overcome any obstacles. They demonstrate their ingenuity by getting results. It is all about logic—being smarter than other players.

You find chess players in roles such as project leads, managers, directors, and vice presidents. They are not organized in teams, but rather have a role where they are responsible for product teams or a business function. Their success depends upon the results of their teams as well as how good they are in positioning themselves against other leaders in the company.

Even if a group is doing really well, it may be crushed during a budget cut if the manager or leader cannot withstand the pressure from above or it is being surpassed by other groups' abilities to position themselves in the eyes of the executives. Chess is about thinking ahead and envisioning a sequence of events that could lead to a better position. The winning strategy for these players is to anticipate possible failures of the group, as well as new opportunities, and then be ready to act on early signals.

Monopoly Players

Here you have executives, general managers, and other senior managers. They are at the pinnacle of the company's leadership. Combined, they overlook an empire of people, money, and equipment and are responsible for the safekeeping of the net worth of the company and its future. The main difference from the actual Monopoly board game is that this group uses real money and often changes or forgets the rules, especially if there is an advantage to be had in doing so.

Company leadership seeks to grow market share, expand company reach, and crush the competition. This is a game of power. Collectively, this group is playing external Monopoly against the competition. At the same time, they are playing internal Monopoly against one another. This book is focused on internal Monopoly, which is where they place most of their energy and focus on a daily basis. Normally, leaders will show their power by pointing at both external and internal success.

Team versus Individual Games

Playing with blocks or bricks is mostly a team sport where the members have a common goal and most often the main competition is themselves. They are trying to beat their own past achievements and do their job really well. They don't compete directly with other teams, although they do compare success from time to time.

In chess and Monopoly, individuals play against one another. The primary way to win is to beat someone else. Occasionally, you see a leader leveraging a small group of trusted employees, but rarely do you see a leader involve the whole group in playing the game. Sometimes a leader engages his or her group by brainstorming ideas on how to approach the game or how to represent the leader in meetings or events. When leaders do involve their groups, they tend to play the games very well, because they include different points of view and therefore create a better approach to the game. But most leaders rely only upon themselves. They do this since they are always looking for a better position from which to play the game, such as a different role or a new set of responsibilities that may open the door to new opportunities. That may require leaving their old support network behind. Therefore, these players carefully evaluate how much to rely upon others versus what they can do by themselves.

The Rules

If companies had figured out and shared the rules of the games, the benefit would be that everyone would know how to get things done in a more fair and even manner. This results in improved employee engagement and job satisfaction, which again is linked to better company performance. The flip side is that this would limit power and the ability to influence outcomes for those who already have an understanding of the games. Regardless, since most companies are not aware of these games taking place, very little information about them is provided to someone who has just been hired. So, they are left to learn on the job.

Why should these rules be shared? Chiefly, because most people are simply not aware of the dynamics. They may operate within the rules but take it for granted that everyone else knows what they themselves know. So what you end up with is that everyone understands their part, but nobody can articulate the big picture, the collective set of rules. Therefore, nobody can label the dynamics, the games, and describe the rules. This can lead to chaos and bankruptcy. A company with clear and well-managed rules has a much better chance of success.

During the first day in a new company, you may attend several informational sessions to start your integration. You hear about mission statements, goals, customers, groups, and more. Sometimes you get a glimpse of the rules when covering topics such as innovation, priorities, and employee benefits. Perhaps your new manager sits down with you and informs you about the various challenges and the winning strategies. What you normally hear is how to approach certain situations such as making decisions, how to work with certain groups, whom to avoid, and what to say and not say.

Eventually, you get to know your fellow employees and how the organization works. In short, it is totally up to you to collect the rules of the games. I have never seen a clearly defined, complete set of rules for any of these games. I have seen incomplete sets of rules in some groups for certain topics, such as annual planning, setting goals, and giving rewards. The reward system is probably the clearest evidence of the rules. The bell curve for annual bonuses will drive people toward individualistic behavior, regardless of team spirit, and encourage employees to outmaneuver others in order to be rewarded.

Then there are those who have discovered a way to navigate a game. They may not fully understand it, but they have discovered key moves for some situations. For the most part, these people are not sharing the rules. Why would they? They are in it for themselves. Often they will use this knowledge to move on to the next game. We have all heard about someone getting promoted until they reach a level where they perform poorly. Why does that happen? The reason is because they do not understand that the game and the rules have changed. They continue to play the game they knew and therefore will eventually fail when everyone around them is playing a different game with different rules. We label this as incompetence, but it is actually confusion about which game to play.

The main challenge that prevents people from learning the rules of the games is that companies fill their communication channels with volumes of narratives about what is happening in the organization, such as customer success, product releases, industry events, internal initiatives, and social programs. This is designed to support the well-being of the company, its employees, and society. There's nothing wrong with that, but it leaves little space for covering dynamics and how to play the games in a way that is beneficial for all involved. Those discussions are normally had behind closed doors—and you are not invited.

Outcomes

Regardless of the variations across companies, in the end the games are about power, logic, and creativity. Monopoly is about power. Chess is about logic and intelligence, while playing with blocks and bricks is about creativity and solving problems.

In the next few chapters, we will dive into game dynamics and methods for playing the games. Or, to put it in a different way: the rules and how to play to win.

5

Blocks

Playing with blocks or bricks is what the majority of employees are doing. They design, develop, and support products and services, either in project-development teams comprised of employees from many different specialties or from functional groups such as customer support or finance. They are focused on getting their job done and moving on to the next challenge. This is where value creation takes place.

How do you win playing with blocks at work? There are many ways. You can be recognized for delivering a project according to plan. Or perhaps you had an idea for a new feature that was implemented in a product. As a result, you may get a raise and be allowed to work from home. Fundamentally, winning is being part of the team and permission to continue to play with blocks. Losing is not being allowed to play. There are many ways to win, but only one way to lose, namely, you are no longer allowed to play and must leave the company. In this chapter, we will first look at the rules and then discuss options for how to win.

Core Rules

There are universal rules that everyone has to abide by when playing with blocks or bricks. There is simply no way around them. These rules are deeply rooted in how the world works. For instance, you cannot put a two-by-four LEGO brick on top of a column of ten one-by-one LEGO bricks and expect the whole structure to be stable. A small bump will make it fall over. You simply cannot build a one-foot LEGO bridge without long supporting bricks, either.

In the real world, the universal rules are similar, except they are built on the core of human behavior. We all know what good behavior looks like. It may vary from place to place, but it normally includes respect, integrity, honesty, and accountability, to name a few. Most companies declare some of these to be part of their core values. In addition, they may add company values, such as customer focus, community, fearless innovation, and teamwork. By combining people and company values, you get a set of rules that outline the behavior that is expected at work. These are the core rules of playing with bricks on the job. You can try to ignore them, but people will notice and remember your omissions.

Problems arise when employees take liberties with core rules, such as honesty and respect. This puts everyone in a bind, particularly if the person in question is doing great work. Now management and its teams are forced to make a decision: accept the lack of honesty for the sake of great work or value honesty over great work? Often these choices are not that clear-cut. But they need to be resolved, because in the long term, breaking the rules will ruin teamwork and eventually destroy teams and, potentially, the whole company.

Unfortunately, for some managers, breaking rules is acceptable. They plan to exit the company by the time of reckoning. All they need in the short term is to show results and use them as a springboard for their next steps.

Adhering to the core rules is not enough to be rewarded, but it is required for long-term success. Playing with blocks as long as you like is part of that success. Therefore, sticking to the basic rules is a must and, frankly, one of the simpler requirements.

Team Rules

We all like rules that support how we want to get things done. For example, we expect peers to do what is needed without too much debate. We like to assume it is enough to give a team directions once and then check back when all the work is done. But that is not how the world works.

The problem is that when we, as people, think about desired rules, they often conflict with the real world. If I had a choice, I would prefer a team with no conflicts, and every time I speak, the team stops what they are doing, listens, and then applauds. Of course, I have not found this team or place yet. Instead, I always seem to find teams with a set of rules that are created in an imperfect world, resulting in rules that are not ideal. At least, that is my experience.

We all can feel frustrated by events at work. But if you can't overcome feelings of hopelessness, it may lead you to seek greener pastures in different team or company. Or, said in a different way, you are looking for a team with rules that you like better.

But we have choices. Leaving can be one way of finding success. Sometimes, that is the best decision. But before making that choice, think about the costs. It takes time to get in the door, to find a new team, to become accepted, and then achieve success. So before leaving, make sure you have exhausted every opportunity at your current place of work.

Another path to success is to learn and accept the team rules. Ponder what they will allow you to do and what opportunities they can provide. Be aware of placing limits on yourself, such as, I am not experienced enough or there are other people who can do the job better. It is critical to not mingle these self-imposed limits with the core block rules. These rules are enforced by others, while your one personal limits should not be holding you back.

Back to the team rules: Each set of rules, or accepted behaviors, exist as a result of one or more leaders practicing their management philosophies. Rules also change over time, but they never disappear. The rules may vary across teams, or they may be fairly consistent throughout the company. Regardless, the better you understand them, the easier it will be for you to play with blocks or bricks.

Team rules drive team behavior in every way. Understanding them gives you the insight into why these rules are in place and which ones are more important than others. A team with a specific set of rules is bound to operate in a certain way, and this behavior tends to repeat. That is your opportunity: understand the rules, and let them work in your favor. That will allow you a better chance at predicting the future, to foresee and rank possible outcomes.

You may challenge some of the rules, and you may choose to accept others. It all depends upon what will provide better results for a given situation *and* for your long-term success. Regardless, it is important to recognize that what happens at work is not about you. We often interpret events as if they were designed to cause us harm. They are not. Playing with blocks or bricks at work is not about any one person. It is about the bigger picture—and what you can contribute to the system.

Categories of Team Rules

There are many types of rules at work. I have encountered a broad range of them. For the longest time, I have been trying to understand the different sets of rules and which approach could provide the best results.

While working for Apple, my role was to help teams that had gotten themselves into trouble or faced a challenge. I quickly had to understand a team's dynamics in order to provide the appropriate level of support or, in some cases, suggest changes. If I approached every team as a totally unique system, it would take a long time to address the situation. So I started to look for commonalties and patterns, then link them to proven approaches. Eventually, I learned to quickly identify patterns, and my ability to help teams improved. But it was not until recently that I was able to organize the rules of playing with blocks into four distinct categories.

I first read about these categories in an article by Gibson Burrell and Gareth Morgan called "Sociological Paradigms and Organisational Analysis," published in 1979. It tries to make sense out of behaviors, particularly what motives are behind behaviors. I have taken inspiration from these categories and provided my own interpretation. I have done this to make it easy to understand what motivates certain teams and how to achieve success in a given situation. Thank you Burrell and Morgan for a great inspiration! The reason these categories resonated so well is that they perfectly describe my own observations and encounters.

The first category I call the Dolphins. These mammals have adapted to life in the ocean over millions of years. They are fast swimmers and effective hunters, use biological sonar for orientation, and communicate frequently using sound (clicks). They are described as very intelligent and curious. But most of all they are social beings. They swim in pods that loosely belong to a larger group. As male dolphins mature they may move into other pods. They form bonds, they squabble and fight. Dolphins may all look the same, but they are really individuals, some even have a signature whistle. Dolphins live within their social boundaries, but everyone takes part in everything the pod does. They hunt together, they play together, and they relax together. There is no larger purpose in life than simply living in the moment.

The second category is best described as Aristotle. He was a Greek philosopher and scientist (384–322 BC). He was one of the earliest contributors to logic theory. Aristotle believed that the greatest human endeavor was to use reason and avoid extremes. This concept is called "The Golden Mean." In other words, apply moderation in all things. Aristotle looked at the world as a logical place where everyone and everything has its place. Therefore (my interpretation), everyone should work well together as a team with common goals.

The third category is Captain Nemo, from the book *Twenty Thousand Leagues Under the Sea* by Jules Verne, published in 1870. In this fictional story, we find a person who has abandoned humankind, society, and any organization. Captain Nemo and his small crew have left society behind to travel the oceans of the globe in an electric submarine called *Nautilus*, which is a hundred years ahead of its time. Captain Nemo's many brilliant inventions could have changed the world for the better, but he kept them all to himself.

The Joker is the fourth category. Every deck of cards comes with two Jokers. These wildcards, or shape-shifters, take on whatever value and suite the holder wants them to have. These cards bring unpredictability. Any card game with Jokers puts pressure on the established rules. As a result, everywhere a Joker goes, there is conflict and struggle.

To summarize, here are the four categories and their view of the world.

- **The Dolphins:** The world is observed from an individual point of view within a social structure.
- **Aristotle:** People are rational. Therefore, groups are meant to work well together.
- **Captain Nemo:** Organizations are bad. Structure prevents human potential; therefore, we must abandon it.
- **The Joker:** Everything is a crisis. Imminent change is needed because of inherent structural conflicts between groups.

The Dolphins

They live in the moment. Everything is about the here and now. They support the pod because it provides security, better hunting, and someone to play with. They may form strong bonds with other dolphins. Or they might find reasons to fight. Their curiosity drives them to explore and may lead them to friendly encounters with humans, But is does not mean that everything is perfect.

Dolphins are like any group of people you would find in any small town. They experience life through their own points of view and approach challenges in different ways. But none of them is driven by any underlying motive that opposes other teams or people. They don't think about creating a project plan for approaching something new. Instead, they stay true to themselves and power on. At the same time, they tolerate one another and participate in joint activities.

This is the most common type of team, where everybody operates in his or her own world, struggling with daily challenges. If you encounter this kind of team, the behaviors, or rules, are all about proving oneself and showing success. Some may have their own personal goals, while others are just dedicated to being themselves. In this group, it is about overcoming adversity regardless of challenges and doing the right thing. Rarely is there any deep-seated hostility or ill will. It may surface, but it is not what makes this team unique. This team is filled with personalities that respond to their own needs first and others' next.

The one situation, hands down, that really reveals the Dolphin dynamic at work is the office move, when a group is relocated to a new environment. In no other situation have I seen individuals being forced so far out of their shells. What on the surface is a rather dull event can turn into turmoil that lingers for years. I remember that while I was at Apple we moved from the open-cube environment in the Mariani 1 building into headquarters at 1 Infinite Loop, which at the time contained a brand-new research and development campus with offices and some cubes here and there. Each group was assigned a section of the building. The new campus had offices that lined a hallway. In a few places, cubicles lined the outer wall, against tall windows facing a calm, park-like setting. Employees had to choose among an office with a window, a cube with a window, or an office with a window facing the hallway. Productivity in the group probably dropped by half for three months prior to the move and two months after it was completed. For years afterward, unhappy employees steamed about their new office location.

Here are some of the rules you can find in this team. I am not implying that they are all present in every team, but some of them are typically present and some are dominant. Those are the ones that drive the behaviors of the team.

- We must all prove ourselves, so take no prisoners. Building is done primarily to show that we know how to solve tough problems.

- We are the only ones who truly know how to build something. We know what we are doing, so we build big and only test in production. We don't have to ask for input.
- Building is all about having fun. We are great—so build anything.
- Sorry, I cannot help you, as I am busy rebuilding what broke yesterday.
- There are only a few people in our group who can decide how to build something. Everyone else must follow their lead.
- We build separately and hopefully never have to combine what we build into one thing.
- We will never stop adding blocks to our structure, regardless of how big it gets, because this is a great work of art.

The effectiveness of such teams varies widely. You may end up with chaos, or you may be lucky to have experience in the team that can help point the way to success. The team's focus is on the personal interests and what each individual can do right now. Any kind of organized approach is not valued. Management is seen as overhead. What drives the world forward is the fuel from energized individuals. Anything in their way must be removed. Anything that delays immediate action is seen as bad, so sidestep the negative and focus on the positive mood of the day.

These teams do not fight against organizational structure, goals, and plans. They simply ignore them. These teams focus on what they like to do right now. They feel fully justified in this approach, because after all, the world is built by and for individuals.

Aristotle

You will know when you encounter teams influenced by Aristotle. They are very focused on following agreed-upon norms, sometimes to a fault. They have learned to appreciate that using tools and processes will make life easier and have replaced many time-consuming decisions by rules. They have defined a set of guidelines for how to get things done. In other words, they have replaced emotional situations with logical rules. The personalities of team members are not suppressed, but the collective behavior is logical and follows normative rules that are focused on team goals. Why do they do this? Because, it produces better results. Less time spent arguing is more time available for getting things done.

No, wait a minute. Is this true? Does a logical team produce better results than other? Is oppressing disagreement a path toward innovation? It depends. It can be. In other cases, it may not produce new product ideas. Regardless of the effectiveness, what I am describing is a belief, a worldview, a set of assumptions that guides behavior.

Logical teams are found in many places. You often see them in industries where the work is very well defined and repeatable. In these cases, the winning teams are those who get the job done the fastest, so why spend time investigating options? It is similar to flying an airplane. Yes, critical judgments and skills are needed, but the pilots and ground crew follow a very scripted play. In fact, the airlines look at each pilot as interchangeable: one pilot is the same as another, within the same rank. If this was not the case, we would all inquire about who is flying the plane and make our vacation plans when the better pilots are in the air. Our lives hinge upon every pilot being qualified to do their job.

Another place where we find logic leading the way is in manufacturing, where the idea is to do the same thing every day, but improve along the way. These teams are following a template to get work done and often have to adhere to industry standards to prove they deliver products meeting defined quality standards. The last thing you want in these environments are individual-focused teams, the Dolphins, changing manufacturing based upon their own untested view of the world.

Interestingly, logical teams also work well when they face really tough challenges, such as developing a new computer operating system. An operating system like Mac OS, Windows, or Linux is one of the world's most complicated and sophisticated creations. A vast number of functions need to be defined, developed, and tested under a prescriptive timeline. It requires a large number of highly educated people communicating openly and clearly at all times. It may take years to complete. The more these teams can remove noncritical decisions from the process, the more time they can devote to tougher challenges. Noncritical decisions are things such as schedules, roles, decision-makers, what tools to use, what processes to follow, and when to get together for meetings.

My experience is that teams taking on complicated efforts don't start out as a logical team. They evolve over time to behave in more deterministic or logical ways. Some see this as bureaucracy, as something that slows everything down, resulting in mediocre outcomes. However, the other way of looking at this is freedom. Once you have applied logic and rules for most common decisions, the more time and effort you can devote to innovation and important challenges. However, this is not the prevailing view when it comes to innovation.

Can you imagine a world without traffic rules? What if people had to make their own judgments? Someone would surely argue that their way of looking at traffic is the best one. If rules were optimized to their liking, they would be able to get to and from work in half the time it takes them today. But that is not the goal of traffic rules. The most important purpose of these rules is everyone's safety. It is crucial that everyone knows them since this knowledge provides a platform for wise decision-making. Without mutual assurance and acceptance of the rules, we would risk our lives every time we drove through an intersection. Drivers who do not obey traffic lights can cause everyone on the road great harm. Following the rules improves the chances for safe travel, which again allows each driver to optimize their experience within the rules. So it is with logical teams. They have accepted a set of rules that allows them to focus on optimizing results.

When Apple developed the first iMac, the project team was led by a program manager who was experienced in rapidly delivering new products. She accepted and followed every development milestone that was already in place. The team did not spend time reinventing what was not important. Instead, they focused all their energy on developing the iMac, and they did it at half the time and with a quality level double that of all other Apple computers available at that time. The iMac became the product that led Apple away from the brink of disaster. The team stayed focused on the real goal and would not allow members to spend time changing defined and functional processes.

The opposite happened a few years earlier when a new project team was created to move the aging Macintosh operating system to a newer platform. All the initial efforts were focused on creating a new way of managing development. For example, every communication was to be done using a central documentation system. No one could send an e-mail to ask a question—everything was to be posted on the documentation system. The idea was to provide everyone insight into everything that was happening across the project. Moving away from emails was therefore important. Close to thirty program managers were moved or hired to help coordinate and facilitate communication. In no time, the project failed.

This is not to say that you should not improve processes. But be mindful of how to approach them. You should carefully assess the cost of changing a system that is in place and how these potential improvements will impact project success. If there is hope for significant improvement, then go for it. But if it is only about getting things aligned with how you would like it, forget it. Logic in this case dictates a focus on optimizing product success. Sometimes that means changing the system; sometimes it means following its rules. Sometimes you are successful, and sometimes not. Logic does not assure success; it just means teams make decisions based upon the best available information rather than allowing the Dolphins to swim wild.

In all these teams, individual behaviors are still present. That is fine. The best use of different points of view is when making decisions, such as what feature to develop and what market to approach. Aristotle-influenced teams typically display a strong sense of reason and purpose that keeps the inner *Dolphin* members in their pods. Collectively, they operate for the most part according to their logical set of rules. Here are some examples of their rules, which simply boil down to, "The Golden Mean."

- A project follows a very well-defined process where information is made widely available. There is very little outside interference, as everybody knows who is in charge and how decisions are made.
- We build as a team.
- A product can ship only when every criteria is met. No exceptions.
- Team members are allowed to fill their roles as best as they can.

Very little bickering among employees is tolerated.

- The focus is on customer problems and a reasonable solution, given time and cost parameters.
- There are clear rules for how a team is awarded.
- There is a wide understanding of why the team exists and how it relates to other teams. Each team may have different goals, which is OK, but collectively, they all support the bigger goal.
- Building is about solving customer problems, so let's at least talk to some of them.

In summary, what drives Aristotle teams are facts, purpose, reason, and logic. This behavior limits wide swings in individual behavior. It is expected that everyone works as part of a team and focuses on their role and end goals.

Captain Nemo

The Aristotle team is in stark contrast to the next group of teams characterized by Captain Nemo. Although his country of origin was never revealed, Captain Nemo spoke many languages. After some unexplained altercations with society, he quietly escaped into the world's oceans with a small and very dedicated crew. Captain Nemo traversed the globe exploring and capturing data to better understand the oceans he lived in. Along the way, he had encounters with ships that created a worldwide stir and led many nations to hunt his *Nautilus* with the intent to destroy it, believing the submarine was a large beast that posed a threat to humankind.

Captain Nemo's many inventions, such as the oxygen tank and diving suit, made it possible for him to reach places no other human could go. As a result, he found riches beyond his needs. His view of the world was a mix of superiority and disdain for nations, organizations, and other groups. He was not against humans, but rather how they collectively had offended him. He did not want to play by anyone else's rules and instead created his own. Captain Nemo was an explorer and scientist, constantly seeking new knowledge. In the face of danger, he was brave and looked out for his crew.

If you encounter a team with the Captain Nemo spirit, you will know immediately. This is a team that sets its own rules and its members think of themselves as invincible. It will be full of bright individuals who have been successful in the past. They receive the respect of other teams and senior leaders. There will be one strong leader that the team fiercely supports. This kind of team is willing to take chances and break new ground. They are also willing to leave other organizations behind in their quest for new ideas and better solutions. They are typically close-knit and do not like intruders.

What sets this team apart from others is its total abandonment of organizational rules and the distance it keeps from other teams. A Captain-Nemo team separates itself from the larger organization and does not seek acceptance from others. This team's members will fiercely defend against any attempt to limit their abilities to do what they decide is the best course of action. In short, they have left dry land and are cruising the oceans in their own invincible submarine.

The rules these teams follow may vary, as each submarine crew will be different, but here are some that are common.

- Through suffering, we arrived at a view of the world that will allow us to create technologies and solutions far beyond anybody else's capabilities.
- We don't owe anybody anything.
- We are capable of doing whatever we want.
- Rules are for everyone else. Our own abilities will not be restricted by following the larger group's methodologies.
- Build small, then validate. Learn. Then build bigger. How big can we build?
- The best product wins. Everyone is encouraged to experiment with any type of blocks or bricks and build any structure.
- Do not touch our blocks!

These fiercely independent teams will shield their members from the rest of the company. Loyalty is critical. If you belong to this team, you are given a wide range of options to do great things. It is a supportive environment, because it is the success of the group that allows it to remain independent. That is a powerful motivator that drives the team forward.

The drawback of these teams is first the inability to direct their efforts, and as such, they may run counter to the organization's goals. The other is that the rest of the organization feels punished for following the rules while the Captain Nemo team gets away with anything. Because of this, the most common use is to create these teams for a shorter period of time with very specific goals. Words used to describe them could be Tiger or SWAT teams.

The Joker

The need for excitement drives the Joker. Excitement is found in chaos, and that is easily created when something breaks or groups collide. When different ideas compete, chaos can easily ensue. The Joker is unstable, but he is also a genius. He looks at the world as a place that must change, must be destroyed to meet his desire for making an impact. As such, he has difficulties working with anyone for a long period of time. Therefore, his team members change frequently.

Like the Captain Nemo team, a Joker team also distances itself from the larger organization, but is actively out to destroy the current world order instead of avoiding it. The Joker does not seek to improve himself or discover new knowledge. That is in stark contrast to Captain Nemo, who wants to escape from society and any organized group, but at the same time is a scientist endeavoring to expand his realm of knowledge.

A team with the Joker spirit lives in constant change. Each day is a new day, with yesterday forgotten. They look to seize any opportunity to get things done. These teams are not afraid to make changes or create conflict to get what they want. For them, other teams do not matter. They are there as a backdrop. If needed, they can be sacrificed for the fun of it.

A Joker team is not content to play within its own borders. Team members are always craving opportunities to engage. A typical example is when the larger group identifies a problem. Perhaps there is a spike in customer complaints, a project missed its delivery date, or a new initiative is proposed. A Joker team quickly jumps into the action by offering to solve the problem. Within days, its leader will define a solution and send out a meeting invite to a larger number of people. The team will not spend much time investigating the options to select the best path forward or reaching out to all involved parties to gather information. Instead, in the meeting it will declare that the organization has a problem and inform everyone that they are all responsible, therefore they should fix it. They will set a short deadline for the other teams and then leave the meeting. They will follow up with an e-mail to executives that the problem has been solved. All that is needed now is that the other teams deliver. And if they fail, that is not the Joker team's problem.

What happened here? The Joker team introduced chaos into the organization and handed over accountability to everyone. At this point, the number of questions left unanswered and the level of confusion makes progress close to impossible. Most often than not, new problems arise in other areas as a result. This shifts the focus away from the original problem, allowing the Joker team to claim that they solved it and should be rewarded. Not only that, their efficient way of solving the problem also revealed new problems and incompetence in other teams. Naturally, this means that the Joker team should be given an even broader set of responsibilities than before. In short, they are out to undermine other groups and break down an organization's current structure.

If you work on a team like this, here is what you can expect to see.

- Ship on time. Regardless of what is built, it must ship on time. It doesn't matter if anybody wants it or if it works. It just needs to ship on time.
- I will not tell you what to build, but I expect it to be delivered on time.
- Change will happen, so get used to it.
- Every day is a new challenge. Expect a constant string of changes and surprises every day you go to work.
- Planning ahead is not important, as plans will change. Instead, we will react quickly when change happens.
- Build the product and show me. Then I will decide if it is good.

- We will never be given enough time or resources to do what we want, so we have to step up our efforts. New challenges bring out the best in people and show others what we are made of.

If you thrive upon action, then the Joker will provide all the excitement you can handle. These teams offer growth opportunities and new challenges. They also demand that you buy into a worldview that is about operating inside a storm, where the purpose is to survive, not build structures that will weather future storms and benefit other citizens in town. Surprisingly, this is a path that many people prefer to take, as it can bring about instant success with little effort. That is the essence of creating chaos.

Success Is Built upon Core Values and Team Rules

To summarize, there are two sets of rules that you need to be aware of when playing with blocks or bricks. The first is the core value set (human and company values), and the second is a set of rules imposed by a specific team or group. Each set is different, but success requires full awareness of all rules that are being enforced at any given time.

Once you have obtained the list of rules, you have choices. The first choice is to accept the rules and play within their boundaries. If you do this, the next question is whether you can be successful in that environment. If you are good at creating new processes but the team hates process, what do you do? Do you have other skills that can make you successful? If not, then success may not be possible, and it may be time to leave. That is, in essence, your second choice.

If you do decide to stay, you can challenge the status quo by breaking or redefining a few rules. You may find that these changes will benefit the team and give you success. Or you can operate within the rules and focus your efforts on what is possible to achieve. If the team allows individuals to drive change and you have many new ideas, then look for the Dolphins. If you are more comfortable with a strong team with a rational approach, join an Aristotle team.

Success Behaviors

Rules and awards aside, in addition to the core societal and company values, there are some behaviors that I have found to be universally fundamental for success in every organization I have come in contact with. If you consistently practice them, you will be successful at playing with blocks or bricks. At the same time, remember that you also have to do your best in your current role. You don't have to be the best at it; you just have to do your best.

Of all the key success behaviors, there are two I have found to be lynchpins for success. They are easy to comprehend and if you focus on them, you can quickly learn to skillfully apply them. You don't have to be the best at adhering to them; you just have to consistently apply them. I determined what these two assets were after ten years of being a team manager. I was constantly looking for a simple and concise way of assessing a person's impact on product development. In the end, it was clear that long-term success is not primarily about someone's interpersonal skills or knowledge, but rather about how they interact with other team members. That is shown primarily through two behaviors.

- Creating win-win scenarios whenever you can.
- Building and maintaining good personal relationships.

The great thing about these two behaviors is that there are many books written about how to build relationships and make a difference at work by becoming a problem-solver. You may have your own list of skills that you have validated through the years. If so, apply them as well. However, before doing so, be sure that they are not focused on you as the only benefactor. These behaviors must benefit the world around you in order for you to leave a lasting impression and create new opportunities for you and others. If all you do is take from the teams, your luck will quickly run out.

Here are my views of the two success behaviors and how you can implement them to pave the way for your success.

Win-Win

It is easy to be lazy. It is a trap to assume that you can be yourself and the work will just get done. Being yourself is not sufficient. The problem is that at work, nobody should be him- or herself.

Let me explain. At work, I don't want to be myself. Instead, I want to be someone who does his best within my given role. If I wanted to be myself, I would stay home, go fishing, and have long lunches. At work, I have a job to do.

I am not advocating that you not be true to yourself and your values. I am simply stating that work is not the same as personal time. Work is defined as using your skills and time to create value in exchange for money. That leaves you with one big decision to make: does this job matter to you? If no, then leave. Otherwise, do your best. That does not mean you put forth effort now and then. It means you put forth effort all the time. Every time you engage with someone, you look for a way to create a win for him or her. The great thing is that if they associate you with a win for them, that is also a win for you.

It is easy to create wins. They require almost no extra effort. All they take is a mind-set of looking for them. Don't forget that even the smallest effort can result in a big win. Let's explore a few examples.

Take notes: If you attend a meeting with many people and nobody seems to take notes or create a short list of key action items, then volunteer. You are there anyway. Why not control history by holding the pen? Do not let such an opportunity go to waste. Everyone will thank you. Having something to show for spending an hour in another meeting has value for most people.

Follow up: If you say you will do something, then do it. Never let light come between your words and your actions. You are your actions, not your words. If you keep the shadows away, you will build a reputation as a solid and reliable person who can always be trusted.

Make a decision: How much time have we spent debating topics without making any progress because we did not have all the right information? Teams can take forever looking for perfect data to make perfect decisions. Most consider not making decisions a waste of time. Therefore, make one. It does not have to be a big decision. It can be as simple as deciding who will take the next step by when. The fact that there is a concrete plan (even if it is simple) is always appreciated. Therefore, do not add noise to an issue. Instead, show the team a way out.

Offer to help: Sometimes that is all it takes. Someone is stuck or running out of time. Perhaps something as small as sending an e-mail to follow up on a question is all that's needed. Sometimes all you have to do is listen. If you have a choice, extend a hand.

Take the lead: Don't look around for new opportunities on the other side of the company. Look first at your own group. There is always something that is missing or can be improved. Propose that you lead change. It can be anything. Start small by offering to send out a group newsletter once per quarter. Be the one who organizes the next fun group event. Come up with something new that people will remember. Put some effort behind it to make it great. Prove your abilities on something small. The next time a bigger opportunity comes around, management will look your way.

All these behaviors will make you appear as someone who solves problems, someone who can help and get results. The more success you are connected with, the more layoff-proof you will be. But, more importantly, the easier it will be for your managers to recommend you for bigger and better things.

Relationships

Relationships are easier if your mind-set is win-win. People gravitate toward those who can help them and make them successful. But you can't create wins that leave people around you exhausted or feeling like they just stepped into a hurricane.

First, make your presence a personal statement. Show that you value other people, that you care, that you are willing to help, and that you're fun to be around. There is only so much criticism and negativity a person can take.

Here are some typical work behaviors that foster relationships.

Be on time: It is easy to slip into a state where time does not have value. So whenever possible, show that you value other people's time by thanking them for starting and ending meetings punctually. Even better, run your meetings so they finish before the scheduled end time. Some meetings are set up at thirty-minute intervals. Most meetings are close to an hour. Make it your goal to end early. Let participants know that you value their time and that you are doing your best to minimize your demand for their presence.

Respond to every e-mail you receive: Yes, we all get inundated with e-mail and requests for our time. It is easy to get bogged down in it; however, it is also easy to find a system to manage your time spent on e-mail and the tasks it produces. You have to use your e-mail software's features and a disciplined approach to solve this challenge. In a world where we rely upon e-mail so much, it is not acceptable to let your reputation be sullied by e-mail chaos. There is nothing more telling about a person's lack of willingness to work with others than failure to reply to critical or time-sensitive e-mail. Of course, I am not referring to marketing or unsolicited emails.

Be present: Pay attention to people when they speak. Make eye contact and engage. Minimize e-mail and phone tasks while in meetings. People will not tell you directly, but when you are on your phone, you are showing that you care less about what is taking place in the meeting compared with your own priorities. When you attend a meeting, that is your priority. If not, don't attend. And most of all, don't drown out the conversation with your tapping keyboard noises.

Be positive: Don't complain. It is easy to point out what is not working and what other people are doing wrong. That is basic human nature. It is also a great bonding experience with like-minded people, for it can be fun to poke at a world that is not perfect. However, at work you have a role, and I am certain nobody hired you to spread misery. If you don't like something, either get over it or suggest corrections. After all, a job is not about you as a person: it is about how you fill your role. Become a problem-solver, a person who brings value to others.

Support the team: Don't allow others to fail. This is similar to not complaining. The only difference is that sometimes you have to listen to what other people have to say about their challenges. That tells them that you care and will help them overcome their current crisis. Sometimes this may not directly benefit you, but in the long run you will be seen as invaluable.

Ask others for help: People like to help. Being asked for assistance puts them in a position to extend their range of influence or knowledge, and that is something that makes people feel good. If they have helped you once, they are more likely to help you again. However, do not ask for help so much that they start seeing you as incompetent.

In the end, relationships are about choices. You can decide to build relationships that will help either everyone or only yourself. The latter choice is a sure way of not getting what you need. So the choice is really easy: build and maintain great relationships at work.

Playing to Win

Winning at playing with blocks is to be able to keep playing, having fun, solving problems, and changing the world. Winning is playing with blocks at any level you want for as long as you want. Everyone who plays is a winner as long as they can contribute at their own levels of ability. So the main question is, at what level do you want to play? Being aware of the rules at work will make this easier. Knowing what drives teams and people around you will enable you to play a better game: you will have a better understanding of how to approach the game, what options to pursue, and which ones to drop. The more time you spend fighting the rules, the less chance you have for success. If you can, play within the rules. Only break them if it is worth it.

Block Forces at Work

I will end this chapter by reexamining three of the forces that I described in chapter 1. These situations are typical for block or brick players.

> **The promotion:** *The best programmer and engineer is promoted into management. This often happens in high-tech or creative organizations where the value of management is low and managers are expected to be working managers (building products and solutions in addition to managing teams). Unfortunately, if the new manager ends up being your manager, your job is now turned into a competition. Your manager is constantly showing you that he or she still has it. In the process, your boss forgets to manage the team, and you suffer.*

In this very typical case, a great block player has been promoted. When this occurs due to the person's ability to work well with others and influence outcomes, all is well. That is what a manger should do. The problems pile up when the person's main skill set is building new things. That ability may not translate into being a great manager. A new manager often remains very involved in building with blocks, sometimes to the point of making all building decisions, because now that manager has all the power. Some companies expect a first-level manager to be a "working manager," someone who is also building products or playing with blocks. This makes the distinction between being a manager versus being part of the team even more challenging and confusing. Think about kids. A parent is first a parent, then a friend. So it should be at work, a manager's job is to first and foremost make the team and team members successful.

If the new manager is the Joker or Captain Nemo, get ready for a wild ride. Both have demonstrated that changes can be made, but in a way that most people avoid. When working for Aristotle, you know the rules will be simple and clear. Roll the dice if you end up working for any representative from the Dolphins. The clicking sounds may drive you crazy or you may love surfing the waves.

The main challenge in this particular situation is that the new manager still plays with blocks. Why does that happen? And why do you have to suffer, in the sense that you don't get a manager who will help you and the team be successful? The main reason is that the person behind the promotion decision did not fully understand, or appreciate, that the new manager was moving from playing with blocks to playing chess. Playing chess is very different than playing with blocks. And to make it worse, most likely the new manager was not informed about the rules for chess. So it takes trial and error before the new manager starts to understand the new rules and how to play the game.

The desperate team: Your development team is frustrated that product management is constantly changing priorities. You can't understand why making decisions is so difficult. Nothing gets done. No success is in sight. Before long, the whole team is doing nothing but complaining about everything. How did it come to this?

If you have been part of developing new products, you may have been on a desperate team—a place full of complaints and where everything is wrong, particularly management and other groups. The team's mood may be pleasant enough, but nothing seems to ever get done. Instead, there is endless discussion about why things do not work. How can this be?

This is primarily a team that builds products or plays with blocks. They enjoy clear direction, accept tough challenges, and are fine with doing hard work. But they shy away from indecision and lack of success. In some sense, we all probably do. But this situation is not good when it impacts the team's ability to engage in meaningful work. The problem here is that someone is using the team as a pawn in their own chess game, likely the first- or second-level managers. They are hoping the team will create more value than it currently has. They are looking for better assignments or perhaps more resources. Meanwhile, the team has no direction and support, and without them, success cannot be achieved.

I see this as a management failure. A manager always knows what to do. They are paid to make decisions, even if they do not get clear instructions from executives. They always have to keep in mind that a team playing with blocks must always play with blocks. Preventing them from playing is failure. So regardless of uncertainties, management must give clear instructions to their team. It can be as simple as deciding that in the next two weeks, the team will do task A and then review its progress. It cannot be left as management having no idea what to do and planning to change direction every week. Yes, the team may face real challenges outside their control, but this is where management muscles are built. If the team is not engaged, it will remain desperate and eventually cannot recover. The only remediation then is to disband the team and have the members start anew with other teams.

> **The troubled employee:** *An employee who is unable to find the right team reaches out to executives to ask them to fix his problems. They offer support and decide to move the employee into a new role. But after a while, the problem-employee returns to them, saying he still feels that nothing has changed. According to him, the executives do not know how to run the company. What is going on here?*

In every company, there are always employees who see the sky as falling. They have great ideas about how the company should operate and will boldly exclaim how everybody around them is doing everything wrong. They may have ended up in this position after years of suffering defeats or lack of success. Or it can simply be that their glass is half-empty. Either way, they will gladly talk to anyone who is willing to listen.

Their stories are normally put together well. They will spend all their time creating a future version of the world that will never materialize. Mostly, these futures center on the assumption that everybody else will be following their lead. They conveniently step over facts, such as the one that leading positions are earned, not granted. Being a leader is something you grow into, unless your mother owns the company. But then, that person is probably not reading this book, so they are doomed to perpetually seek something that will never materialize. Hence, they move around and engage every team in how the world should work versus what is being done today. In other words, they are totally unaware of the block rules. In order to become successful, they have to be aware of them and either follow them or combat them with a purpose. Rewriting the fundamentals of block rules is not easy, as they are cemented in human nature.

Next Steps

By now, I hope that the insight into the block rules has given you a different way of looking at the forces at work that gives meaning to seemingly unexplainable events. With this view you can now start engaging more effectively with other block or brick players. Now, with this mind-set, let's take a look at chess, a game about outmaneuvering other players.

Erik N. Boe

6

Chess

Most employees play with blocks, organized into teams that are inventing, selling, and supporting products or services. Teams are formed because it is simply impossible to do all this work alone. They are organized into groups and then into larger groups, or divisions. The bigger the group grows and the higher in the management structure that one ascends, the less one plays with blocks and is affected by block rules. Occasionally, you see teams at a higher level in the organization playing with blocks, but that is rare. It will only be because the company is still small, perhaps a start-up. Or the team is protected by someone higher up the executive chain—a Monopoly player. For the most part, managers who have managers reporting to them are playing chess.

The dominant behavior among managers is to seek advantages that result in a better position than before, as compared with other managers. Being in a better position opens doors for greater opportunities and better rewards. Some managers seek to *win* the game by advancing to Monopoly and end up as CEO. But most are striving to simply improve their current position or move on to an even better one. Of course, many events outside their own influence will impact their advancement and may even lead to removal from the game altogether. Sometimes these events are predictable. Sometimes they come without warning.

In short, a manager in corporate America is playing chess. The typical chess player is an individual manager playing against many other managers. Rarely do you see a team of managers uniting to play against other individual managers, but it can happen. Let's now take a look at how chess is typically played at work.

Learning the Rules of Chess

How is chess played at the office? Where are the rules found? Unfortunately, they are not written on paper or stored in an electronic file; they are passed down in our genes from generation to generation. The rules are as old as humankind. They are about self-preservation. It is about the accumulation of wealth, the removal of threats, and finding safe harbors. We are all born with a desire to seek positions that lead to these outcomes.

We as humans have evolved to be able to process, store, and recall memories in a way no other life form can. This unique ability enables us to envision the future. Based upon what we have learned, we can quickly assess if a situation is similar to something we experienced in the past. We then use these memories to predict possible outcomes. The more outcomes we can think of, the better the chance that we will find one that will work to our advantage. If one option is not successful, we can always choose another. The ability to predict the future improved our ancestors' chances for survival. Hence, the chess game comes naturally to us.

This behavior is brought to the front and center in companies due to how work is organized. A typical approach is to keep employees who do the same work in the same group. But when the organization grows, you have to break the group into smaller groups, each with a manager. Naturally, this creates a competitive situation. Another way of organizing is around a larger purpose where employees with many different skill sets are placed into teams, so collectively they can achieve the group's goals. This also creates a competitive situation, as the group will compete with other groups that have different goals.

Some of us are better than others at constantly looking into the future. I read a book once about a politician who said that when he entered a room he immediately categorized people into three types: who can hire me, who can help me, and who can get me fired. This is kind of how chess is played—you constantly look for opportunities and threats.

It is not easy to decipher the dynamics of a perpetually moving organization. New players will impact the game. When players leave, you may lose your support system and become open to attacks. When a new business challenge comes around, it may affect your group. Staying ahead of all these changes is tough work.

A chess grandmaster will have spent a significant amount of time to achieve this title. On the average, it takes three to four hours a day for at least eight to ten years. It is not enough for a grandmaster to understand the rules. He or she must constantly practice so he or she can recognize an almost endless set of game combinations and what they have to offer. The grandmaster must be able to memorize a large number of past events and recall them to help envision the future. The more possible outcomes a player can envision with every move, the better player that person will become.

So it is at work. The many players create an almost endless set of possible outcomes. The more exposure you get to different situations, the better player you will become. Therefore, the best advice is to always seek new situations that will challenge you.

Let's take a look at some common chess situations at work. I used fictional characters to describe the block or brick players. I did that because when playing with blocks it is primarily a players' own limitations that influence how blocks are used and the outcome of the building activity. In describing chess, I will use the chess pieces themselves to outline manager characteristics. I do this because each chess piece has strict rules on its movement. Or said in another way, it is very predictable.

The King

The game of chess ends when the king is captured. Without him, the other pieces have no power. Note: at work the characteristics of a king can be embodied by both men and women. The same is true for the queen and other pieces. Moving on, the king cannot move fast or far, and as such is not an offensive player. You can use the king to neutralize your opponent's move, but for the most part the king has to be heavily defended. On the flip side, if you try to attack the opponent's king, you will face heavy opposition and will most likely lose pieces in the process.

At work, you find kings as leaders of the more profitable or critical business groups, such as the one that produces the company's flagship product. Without this group's success, the company would not be in business. Whatever this group wants, it gets. Its leader knows this, so he or she does not have to move very swiftly or pose any direct threat to any other group or leader. The leader knows that if anyone attacks, he or she will be strongly defended by others. In product development companies, you rarely find kings in supporting groups, such as customer support, technical documentation, finance, human resources, and internal IT divisions. These groups are there to support the core product groups. Of course, depending upon the industry, the power groups will vary.

Playing against a king is not advisable unless all of your other pieces are lined up behind you and the opponent's pieces are not nearby to defend the king. Getting into this position will probably not happen until you have gained a few years of chess experience.

A king may leave the game, the group, or the company. When that happens, the whole organization must rebuild ties to the new king. In the process, the power shifts around and creates new opportunities for many managers.

The Queen

The queen can move fast and far in any direction. She can come from out of nowhere and knock you out of the game. Her main purpose is to defend the king, but she is also a very strong offensive player. At work, a queen is found near a king, often in the same group. She is given power to implement or drive change on behalf of the king. Very often the queen has an outgoing, strong personality and great influencing skills. She does not need to be very strategic and look ahead for new strategies or goals, but if she does, she may be looking to take over for the king. The best advice is to avoid a direct confrontation with a queen. Instead, use other tactics to forward your position.

Rooks

Rooks move forward, backward, left, and right. Once a rook is set in motion, he keeps going. He likes simple and clear approaches, for he is not very good at making subtle changes in direction. Nothing goes through a rook since he is built of stone, built to last. You can find rooks anywhere in the organization, and you will know what they want. They are sure of themselves and run their group as their own private army. Their willpower seems to make everything happen around them. They can outline great reasons for why change is needed and are good at defending their own position, so when a rook is coming your way, it is time to step aside. The most efficient way to beat a rook is to redirect them to attack someone else. Stand aside and let the battle play out. When time is right, step in and push over the exhausted rook. An interesting observation about rooks is that should they leave an organization, what is left behind typically crumbles. Chaos follows in the vacuum of a dominating leader.

Bishops

Bishops do not follow a straight path. These pieces move diagonally across the chessboard and therefore avoid many of the traditional obstacles that other pieces face. Bishops look at the world from many different angles and have ideas and solutions that surprise others. They are fearless and can move fast. Like the queen, they can seem to come for you out of nowhere.

Because they spend much time observing the world around them, bishops often land in critical positions in the organization, such as leaders of the budget group, managers in operational groups who coordinate the efforts of many other larger groups, and chief of staffs. They understand who all the other players are and how the game is played. They are pleasant to be around and offer help whenever they can. They normally avoid big battles. Instead, they are more than happy to help others or support initiatives if it benefits their position.

Knights

Knights are the only figures that can jump over other pieces. Every other piece can be blocked by an opponent's piece, but this does not stop a knight. Mounted on a horse, they can leap over and land on a square that is surrounded by opposing pieces and still be a threat. They are fearless attackers. Nothing stops them from a fight but their own distance from it.

You can find knights everywhere in the organization. They are strong individuals who are more than willing to push boundaries. Sometimes they do this with the hope that their sudden and frontal attack will take you aback. This move works on less experienced players, but not on someone who has been in the organization for a while.

Knights are easy to spot. They have a simple and often deterministic approach. If you can stomach their initial attack, they are easy to outmaneuver, simply because many of them rely too heavily upon their first move. They don't have a second move to follow up with. Instead, they repeat the first one over and over, hoping that their brawn will win the game. All you have to do is to take a step back and let them exhaust themselves, or line up a few pieces to neutralize them.

Pawns

Pawns are everywhere. In chess they comprise half of your given pieces. Their ability to move is very restricted unless they reach the other side of the board and are granted the forces of a queen. This can be a powerful motivator for pawns.

A pawn at work is someone who does his or her job and just wants to stay out of trouble. They don't have big plans or spend much time building their network to grow their influence. They are simply content to get things done and support their teams or groups. That has probably been all of us at some or other time in our career. When you get ready for a life-changing event, your focus will naturally be on that very important part of your life. Or when you are starting your career, you may just be happy to find and maintain a job for a while. In any case, a pawn is a reliable and supporting manager who is looking out for the best interests of his or her group and for the company at large. The best approach in all cases is to get to know as many of them as possible and maintain a good working relationship.

Success Behaviors

I have discussed the abilities of various chess players. Each looks at the game from a different perspective and brings unique skills and goals. As you interact with them, it is important to try to understand what player you have at your chessboard. Every kind of player may not be participating in the game. Perhaps you are playing against nothing but rooks? Either way, the approach to the game is the same: maintain or improve the possibility of a better position. That could be more responsibility, a more critical role, better compensation, or a better job title.

In the actual game of chess, there are many strategies you can employ, such as repeating attacks from past games that were successful, utilizing certain types of moves, or simply analyzing each move your opponent makes. In chess at work, there are some approaches that I have found are critical regardless of your playing style. Here they are.

- Demonstrate real success often and broadly.
- Align your goals with important company goals.
- Obtain meaningful executive support.

Demonstrate Real Success Often and Broadly

Nothing, and I mean nothing, will bring you success like success. And therefore, you cannot be successful without it. I like good intentions and applaud good work. They are necessary, but not a sufficient criteria for success.

Lack of success is the shortest way to a group's demise. If your group at any point comes under pressure, then lack of success can easily bring it down. If decision-makers cannot agree that your group is what they need for the overall success of the company, then your group's skillset or level of teamwork will count for nothing.

Never be under the illusion that your team or group is immune. You may be under the king's protection today, but one swift chess move can change all that. Therefore, always look to demonstrate real success. Real success is not the same as knowing that you exist. Sharing information about a new team member, travel policies, and reaching milestones are great, but really, does that matter? We all work in organizations that are filled with information. Just look at your email inbox.

Sharing information to justify your group's existence is also annoying. Constantly reminding others that you have a roadmap, that you attend important conferences for the company, or that you meet your budget goals, are all signs that you lack focus. Success is not defending what you have and what you are expected to do. Success is more than that. Success is making a difference in a big way that is important for the company.

If you lead a team or group, you must be able to demonstrate regular progress toward important goals. You do this by focusing on what is important. You cannot let the daily noise of the work distract you. Teams often race toward the end goal with little or no time devoted to showing success along the way.

So how then, can a team show incremental success? Break down big deliverables into smaller pieces. For example, your team may refuse to release an early version of its product on the basis that it is not complete, explaining that it is missing features or that the marketing strategy is not completed. Instead, they are racing toward a perfect product sometime in the far distance. They are not considering that slowing down, preparing, and supporting early releases will send strong signals that the product has value even if not perfect. Release consistently and you build a track record. In addition, you expand the group's skillset in delivering and supporting products, so when the time comes for the big release, the team is ready to support it. In other words, your chances of long-term success dramatically increase because you already built up goodwill, and your team is ready and capable of dealing with a larger set of customers. Don't let perfection prevent showcasing progress. Find ways to demonstrate success often!

Align Your Goals with Important Company Goals

Alignment means nothing without success. Success means nothing without alignment. You can be the most successful mobile application developer, but that may mean little inside a group of big data analysts.

Your success depends upon knowing what the company values. If you are playing chess in experimental areas, you may never really align with what the company considers important and, therefore, not really be successful.

Finding and taking on critical business opportunities requires skill. It seems easy, but it is not. You don't want to take on a challenge that is too big or is outside your team's area of expertise. Managers, like developers, often underestimate what it will take to get things done, so never promise something you cannot deliver.

You may have to start out small. Deliver something that is part of a bigger solution, but make it great. Make it stand out compared with anything else in the company. Reaching a focused and clear goal in a critical area is more important than solving trivial problems.

Obtain Meaningful Executive Support

That last critical part of success is support from your executives. Someone needs to know that your group is making a difference, or it is just too easy to ignore you when the wind starts howling—and storms are always present in corporate America. It is just a matter of time before they head toward your group.

You may not need your executive to do anything for you or your team, but you need to be on his or her mind. They need to know enough to be able to talk about your efforts in a way that makes them look like they are part of the "in" crowd. That, in turn, will make them a more valuable executive, someone with information about something that is important for the company.

What you really are hoping for is that they will have your back. If someone attacks your efforts, they will defend it. Someone else at the executive level can easily get their priorities placed ahead of yours and therefore eliminate you, regardless of your successes and alignments. Executive support is critical. Personally, I have never been able to achieve success without it.

Playing to Win

What does it mean to win in the game of chess at work? To me, it means that you can continue to play the game and advance both your group and your career at the same time without harming others. Is that possible? Yes.

Staying in the game is about providing value to others and avoiding being eliminated. Doing your best at any time is always important. But you also need to make sure that the value and impact you have continues to be recognized. Constantly look out for changes that make your group less necessary and therefore your contributions invisible. If that occurs, you either need to change the focus of the group or leave it. You should always work with your team or group to make changes in its mission. Team members want to support someone who is looking out for their best interest. So leaving the group should be the last option, because it takes time to find another place and then establish a new network. It also leaves the team exposed to further calamities. Having a history of failed teams is not a winning approach.

The best strategy is to create an environment that fosters collaboration and transparency. This will make it easier for everyone to assess what is going on in the company and take early corrective action. Having a team behind you is a tremendous advantage, so set the expectations for the team that you are there to make them successful. This will, in turn, make you successful. Focusing on only your success is a path fraught with peril.

At the same time, do remain alert to new opportunities. If they are a great career move, then take them. Every company should support career growth. In turn, you should always have a successor in the wings to further support his or her career growth. This will allow you to leave the group on good terms and demonstrate benefits to both the group and yourself. This is a winning approach.

There are many ways you can play the game of chess, but what is the single most important thing you can do to win? Know your opponent. To illustrate this point, let's take a look at what I consider to be the chess match of the last century.

Bobby Fischer versus Boris Spassky, 1972

It was the Cold War. Bobby Fischer and Boris Spassky were from the opposite ends of the world. Spassky was the world chess champion from the Soviet Union. He came from a country where chess was part of the political system; they even had a Soviet chess school. He was backed by twenty-four years of Soviet domination at the world championships. Fischer was the US champion. At the time, the level of chess interest in the United States was modest, so Fischer was not a household name. Due to the limited chess environment in the States, Fischer had to fight for himself to become a chess prodigy.

Fischer and Spassky had played against each other five times before, ending with two draws and three wins for Spassky, who had an aggressive approach and the ability to successfully counter a broad range of playing styles. He was a fierce opponent and the clear favorite to win.

The lead-up to the championship positioned Fischer as the lone American taking on the whole Soviet Empire, an empire that had dominated the chess world for more than twenty years. This setup created great interest. The media was all over the match: newspapers and television shows were making the most of this event. The expectations placed upon Fischer were high. It would be the first world championship to be aired on US prime-time television.

The 1972 World Chess Championship was a lengthy event. It was best of twenty-four games. If the tournament ended with 12–12, the reigning champion would win, since he remained unbeaten. The schedule called for three games per week.

How would you prepare for an event like this? The eyes of the world are upon you while you're getting ready for the game of a lifetime. So what did Fischer do? Did he study Spassky's past matches? Did he attend chess training? Did he play more matches against other grandmasters? Well, here's what happened.

To begin with, there was a disagreement about where to play the game. Fischer wanted it to be held in Belgrade, Yugoslavia (now Serbia). Spassky's choice was Reykjavik, Iceland. They eventually agreed upon Reykjavik. Then Fischer refused to appear at the event if the prize money wasn't increased. A generous donation of $125,000 upped the total winnings to $250,000, an unheard-of amount for this type of event.

In the first televised match, Fischer lost after making a risky pawn grab. This was totally unexpected. Why was he playing so aggressively so early? He lost the second match by forfeit because he complained about the playing conditions: everything about the event's environment was wrong, according to Fischer. At one point it looked like he would forfeit the entire championship. The third game was played in a back room, away from the television cameras, as demanded by Fischer. After that, the game returned to the stage, and the event continued without any other issues.

In the end, Fischer won seven of the next nineteen games. He only lost one and drew eleven. A win gives you one point, a draw ½ point. He won the tournament 12½ points to 8½ points and became the eleventh chess world champion. In the process, the interest for chess in the United States rose significantly.

Fischer won because he knew that he had to approach the game in a way that would unsettle Spassky. He could not allow Spassky to enter the tournament with a laser-like focus on the game, so Fischer created chaos to throw him out of his comfort zone. He knew that the arguments about the venue and prize money would cast doubt about whether the game would take place or not. He knew that his early defeats would put Spassky in an uneasy state of mind. Fischer also knew that moving the game to the back room would create another diversion. After all this, Spassky had lost his focus. Fischer, on the other hand, was ready for the fight. He had planned and implemented diversions without losing focus on the game.

What does all this have to do with winning in chess at work? In short, the winning strategy for chess is to understand your opponent. At work, that means you have to understand who all the other players are and what drives them. You cannot afford to meet the best chess player in the organization and not be prepared. You simply will not win. The approach you take depends upon the situation. Sometimes you unite with other players, other times you avoid them, and if needed you face them. The majority of the time, avoidance is the best approach. If you challenge everyone you meet, your luck will run out. Unite when it makes sense, but be aware of these players' opponents. You automatically become their adversary as well. And finally, take on an opponent when the reward is significant. Don't let your feelings run amok over things that are inconsequential. Save your energy and focus for things that matter.

Chess Forces at Work

Let's return to the forces at work that I described in chapter 1. These are the forces that frequently impact chess players.

> **The new product idea:** *You have a great idea for a new product. You have boundless insight into how to obtain significant market share. You create an excellent presentation that is bulletproof and rehearse it until it becomes a work of art. But less than three minutes into the presentation, the executives shut down your proposal. What went wrong?*

A knight came out of nowhere and knocked your idea out of the game. He had been watching you and your team for a while to see if you posed any disruptions to his plans, and in this case you did. You had entered a space the knight considered his own. Allowing your idea to go forward would create the impression that he was not able do a good job, so the knight prepared. He collected information about your project and added the relevant parts to his own roadmap. Then he compared your current ideas with his. Clearly, he would be able to tell a better story. All he had to do was to claim that his own plan would resolve all the weaknesses in your idea. Then he spoke with a few other leaders to share his roadmap and get their support. As they had not seen your idea, the choice was simple: they gave their support to the knight. When the time came for your presentation, is was pretty much a done deal. Your idea was going nowhere.

Was the knight taking a big risk in this case? Not really. He had the support from others if you wanted to put up resistance, so he was thinking ahead a few moves. He also relied upon the fact that a company is a noisy place that for the most part only looks forward. Not too many people reflect and ponder who promised what last year. Therefore, his approach was very effective and had low risk. This is a very common chess move at work. Let's look at another typical situation.

> **The project cancellation:** *You walk into the office and find out that your project is canceled. The day before, everything was just fine. In fact, it was a model project. Everyone agreed that it was how a project should be run. What happened?*

A rook ran you over. He needed to remove obstacles for his own plans, and he needed resources. Your project was simply ranked as less important than his projects. But to make that happen, the rook first had to spend some time gathering data. He probably linked his project to market growth and product profitability and made sure it was high on the list of internal strategic priorities. He did this by reaching out to other managers and discussing what was important for the company. This is, of course, a very good way of reaching an agreement about the overall intent without personally attacking any one group in particular. The rook used the company's priorities as a way of undermining your project. When the time came to compare where to invest and where to divest, your project did not stand a chance. The fact that your project was in excellent shape did not matter. The rook ran over you and tossed you into the dungeon. Let's consider one more chess move.

The resource ask: *You do a presentation for senior management, but do not make it beyond the first slide. You wanted to ask for additional resources for your project, but instead you leave the meeting with more problems and action items that can fill the next three months. How did that happen?*

A bishop threw a wrench in your plans. He cut across your bow and made you change direction. He also blocked you from moving toward the resource ask. This move requires skill. Not only did he block your request, he also placed the focus on a related, more critical problem and then moved all the attention to that issue. This is possible when faith has been established. Just as a congregation follows the leader, the group at work follows a bishop. He has reached this level of support by building up a string of past successes and favors based upon sound decision-making that has proven to be beneficial for the company. So when he speaks, the group listens. Your resources ask was not aligned with the bishop's motivation. Hence, your reasonable arguments could not compete with faith. You did not have a prayer.

Next Steps

At this point, we have established that the motivations of chess and block players are different, and that fact drives different behaviors. For both sets of players, it is relatively easy to group rules into categories to better understand the current situation and predict future outcomes. I say this because most people are very predictable. They repeat the same moves and for the most part do not hide their motivations. But for the next game, Monopoly, predicting outcomes is much more challenging. In this game, every player knows that it is a power contest, and therefore they keep their intentions hidden.

7

Monopoly

Monopoly is the ultimate game of power. Here you find the winner takes it all, leaving many losers behind. Monopoly can be a vicious game. It is a place where logic and reason do not count for much. Just because someone has a good reason for buying a hotel doesn't mean that other players will like it. If one player's desire conflicts with another's, the one with the strongest position wins. Our primeval part of the brain is what drives this game.

I liken Monopoly players to the many rulers found in medieval Europe. Depending upon their location, their titles could be prince, baroness, viceroy, grand duke, earl, lord, or something else to set them apart from the commoners. A big-enough title indicated if they ruled their own countries or parts of them. Castles with tall stone walls were built to protect them and their big titles. The ideal castle was built atop a hill, surrounded by a village with an outer wall. This two-layer defense made it possible for rulers and their entourages to remain relatively comfortable inside their castles even during a siege. A castle told everyone who was the ultimate decision-maker in that region.

One privilege that came with a major title in medieval Europe was the ability to change your mind at any time, even to the point of acting irrationally. No one could do much about it. Just read a few stories about medieval kings and queens to get an idea of the many intrigues and battles that were rooted in selfish desires. That was then, but we are now in a modern world with modern rules—or are we?

Joining the game of Monopoly is not for everyone. It requires years of preparation. You don't get to be senior vice president of a large company simply because you want to. That only happens if your mom or dad runs the business. That aside, playing Monopoly requires a title—a big one. Not everyone has a desire to play this game or the experience and patience to reach this level. But those who do reach it are skilled and motivated.

The key difference among Genghis Khan, Alexander the Great, and today's Monopoly players is a thin veneer of politeness. Back in the days of Khan and Alexander, a frontal attack was a short way to expand your empire and collect riches. Today, breaking the law to get your way can be punishable by imprisonment. Being a bully and violate office rules can be costly. Therefore, most players have adapted to avoid confrontation with today's many regulatory requirements and laws. There is no point in winning the game only to go straight to prison, lose your job, or be stripped of your winnings. But sadly, there are those who break the rules. Sometimes they get away with it, sometimes not. In some cases it can be a small thing such as parking in the company handicap parking space or a bigger thing such as defrauding the company.

But make no mistake: Monopoly players are smart, motivated, and can be ruthless. They often see themselves as saviors of the group or company. This gives them the ultimate platform for action. They have a reason for winning: they are simply the best. You may be asking yourself, is this really so? Is executive leadership really Henry the VIII reincarnated? And if so, how would you know? Most of the time you don't. Monopoly is a game played behind the inner castle walls. It is not a spectator sport. The way the game is played is just too crude to be exposed. Once in a while, the village will see the smiling ruler and his entourage waving from the castle walls. Perhaps the ruler even pays for a big celebration for everyone with lots of food and entertainment. This is often to secure further support from the village. A successful Monopoly player is very good at public relations. But players are driven by the same desires as kings in medieval Europe—fame and riches.

But is every player really in it for themselves? The answer is yes. However, that neither means that they will not share their winnings, nor does it mean they will hunt you down if you cross their path. I have meet players who are indeed honest and caring, and are looking out for the well-being of the company in addition to themselves. But, they are in the minority. Personally, those are the traits I seek in my manager before taking on a new role. But regardless of their level of altruism, they still have to play by the rules of the game and therefore can be seen as ruthless in certain situations. Say a company has to downsize, someone has to make those decisions. Once you enter the world of Monopoly, you must play the game or leave it. There is no way to sit on the sidelines and become successful. Running a large group forces you to face challenges and opportunities. The amount of decisions and actions needed to be made in larger groups can quickly overwhelm anybody. I have seen a few leaders try to sit in the bleachers and fail shortly thereafter. You are either in the game or you are not. In the game you have to play by the established rules.

Rules

What are the rules of Monopoly a work? The first one is that you have to abide by every legal, ethical, and company rule—in public. The smartest players will also follow these rules in private. They know that if they are skilled, they can win regardless of restrictions placed upon them. Following all the rules makes sense, for it reduces risk. If you don't break any rules, there are no penalties. In addition, you can use that to your advantage to portray yourself as an honest, law-abiding leader and be seen as a role model. But then again, you are a role model who is playing Monopoly.

What follows is a set of timeless principles. By following these rules, you can make decisions to secure your path forward. Break them, and you take your chances. Oppose them all at once, and your path to destruction will be short and swift. Becoming a winner requires keen awareness of what is happening during the game. Here are the ten universal rules for

Monopoly at work.

- The person with the biggest title makes the final decisions.
- The leader of the flagship product gets first pick of resources.
- The best storyteller gets the most time to implement his or her promises.
- The one with the most success gets the first choice of new challenges or opportunities.
- The one best aligned with the CEO gets to be part of the inner circle on setting the direction of the company.
- The one who has the support of the most employees has a great advantage in being consulted before major decisions are made.
- If you fail to deliver, your days are numbered.
- If you cannot defend your position on something you are spearheading, you will never again be trusted or given an important area to manage.
- If you offend a player in front of other players, they will get back at you later.
- If you offend your manager, you will get kicked out of the game.

Let's examine each of these to gain a better understanding of how these rules play out at work.

The Biggest Title

As soon as humankind formed tribes to increase the chances of survival, leaders were appointed. And history is very clear on this: titles matter. It's not so much what a person is called, but rather his or her relative ranking as compared with other titles. History is also clear that the biggest title wins the day.

A person with the biggest title makes the final decisions. One path a leader can take is to make all decisions. That certainly will make that person feel powerful; however, the smarter approach is to delegate as many decisions as possible. That makes life easier for the person atop the pyramid and builds a strong support base with other leaders who are given the authority to make decisions. In any case, the person with the biggest title can always overrule any decision not to his or her liking.

Staying on top is by no means certain. Therefore, it is critical to build a strong inner circle. The leaders in this circle need to be rewarded handsomely. They will not stick close to a big pile of riches if they are not allowed to touch it.

One approach is that the person with the biggest title makes few decisions in public. Instead, the leader makes them in private and delegates implementation to others. The assumption made here is that the less the leader has to demonstrate his or her power, the more support and ability he or she has to move forward. Monopoly players do not like to be told how to play the game, and if the leader lets them play it the way they like, in return, they provide support.

In the game of Monopoly, the person with the biggest title is the one with the most properties and money. They get to make decisions about buying and selling that other players are not able to do. They get to move around the board even if they have to pay taxes to another player. They can afford it. They can easily beat the other players who have less money and therefore fewer options. For the less fortunate players, they may be forced to sell or mortgage their properties verging on bankruptcy.

The Flagship Product

The manager of the group that makes the money also gets to spend the money. No CEO or board of directors is going to jeopardize the money stream. Everything else can be sacrificed before the flagship product suffers.

This position gives the leader free rein to manage the group any way he or she wants. This can also make life difficult for other groups. If the budget is tight, they get less. If resources are scarce, they have to hand them over to the flagship group. In the game of Monopoly, this is equivalent to owning all the expensive properties with a full row of hotels: anyone landing on one of your spaces will have to pay dearly. If an opponent lands on your properties a few times, it will significantly reduce his or her money pile. It is a great position to be in for the hotel owner. As the landlord, you don't have to do much. Just sit back and let other players do the work.

The Storyteller

We all like a good story. Before written language was invented, the stories of our forefathers were carried forth by word of mouth. Then came the written word that enabled details of our past to be shared much more widely across the population. Countless religions rely upon documenting their past in written form. Then came movies, followed by movies with sound. It made storytelling a big business. According to The Statistical Portal, the worldwide box-office revenue will grow from 38 billion US dollars in 2016 to more than 50 billion dollars in 2020.

At work, someone who can tell a good story is always appreciated. If a company is stuck with a particular problem, anyone who tells a convincing story about how to solve it will be heard. Perhaps customers are very unhappy about the level of support they receive. Along comes someone with an approach to improving the quality of customer service. They have data and anecdotal proof that their solution will work. In the absence of competing ideas, they are given the go-ahead to implement their suggestion. As long as progress is made, their story is believed. However, after a while, what typically happens is that the story's promise is not realized, because its premise was not built upon reality.

My firsthand experience with storytellers is that they are supported for no longer than two years. Stories based upon fiction of the past do not change the future—actions do. Great leaders show; they do not tell. They paint a picture of the future. They show what is possible. They inspire.

In contrast, a storyteller places himself or herself at the center of the story. Why? They want to win. They want to acquire a "Get of Out Jail Free" card or advance to Go and collect $200. They may not have a big title, but they hope that their story will result in an upgraded title before their tale runs out of steam. If not, they will quit the game and repeat the story at another company. A new story from the same player will not be tolerated in the same company.

Successes

We all love winners. There is nothing more appealing than someone who can fight injustice and adversity and come out shining. It is a great feeling to be part of an honest win. So it is at work. A leader who has demonstrated that he or she can get things done will be the first in line for new opportunities. Why gamble on someone who has not shown success?

It is the same with Monopoly. If you have shown you can play well, others will be wary of you and will not try to get in your way for fear of retribution. Less successful players may avoid buying a street that a more successful player is eyeing.

Alignment

Being in the center of the inner circle opens doors everywhere in the company. Regardless of his or her official title, this is a position that is noticed. If the CEO and that player seem to act as one, that is a sign of being in the center. At that point, others will pay attention. They may not like it, but they will have to respect it. They will provide support and resources if asked.

In Monopoly, this is like getting support from the player with the most money. Maybe they go easy on you because you are friends or have a connection that other players do not. That is indeed what aligns one to the center of the inner circle.

hold

Support

The difference between support and alignment is that non-players provide support. They watch the game from afar, but they have the ability to influence it. If a player has great popularity and support, that can be very valuable. If that player is asked to leave the company or take on another role, the group could rise in protest or undermine the new leader. Therefore, it is important for leaders to be aware of the level of support someone has before suggesting changes. Monopoly also works this way. Players can gain support from non-players, and that backing can impact gameplay.

Failure

If you fail to demonstrate success—or worse, get pegged with a few big losses—you are in trouble. The tolerance for failure in senior leadership at large companies is small. If you lose big and often, your time will come. It may not be immediate, but you may experience your desk being slowly moved down from the top floor to the basement, and then you're only a small click of the light switch away from complete darkness, like the scene in the 1999 movie *Office Space*.

There are exceptions to this rule. In some companies, a close-knit leadership team can weather failure. This can happen when there is an unsaid understanding of "I fail—you cover me. You fail—I cover you." This can lead to terrible behavior and have a huge effect on a company. On the flip side, it can work great when leaders learn from their mistakes and make the company a better place to be.

In Monopoly, the loss of money and property is a sure road to bankruptcy. Your only chance then is teaming up with someone more powerful.

Defense

Never try to talk knowledgeably about something you do not understand. If there is a problem with a product you manage and someone asks about it, you need to either be on top of it or quickly bring in someone else to handle the inquiry. The last thing you should do is open your mouth and start talking. That is a prime opportunity for other players to expose your incompetence. Remember, they are smart and shrewd. They know what questions to ask to trip you up, which can be as simple as, "What happened?" If you don't know, but others do, you will look foolish. You are the group's leader, not an expert on a particular area. The people who do the day-to-day work will always know more than you about the specifics.

I have seen how the fear of not knowing something resulted in large overhead in status reporting because of the effort to assure others that the company's leaders actually know everything. I have also seen leaders calling meetings in a panic to dive into the details of a problem and try to solve it. They fear being seen as someone who tolerates failure. This, of course, can make the situation even worse. The leader is now attempting to troubleshoot a problem about which he or she knows nothing.

You have to learn to play defense and only talk about what you know. Never admit what you don't know. Instead, state that you will find out and take action to do so. I have seen large groups destroyed simply because the leader said it is not reasonable to expect him to know what his organization was working on. Is it? Yes, it is. Someone is always responsible for everything that occurs in an organization, and that someone is its leader. He may not have all that data with him at any time, but he should be able to quickly find it. Admitting that he does not know at the present time is the same as saying that he did not know in the past, nor does he have the ability to find out in the future. Playing defense means taking responsibility. Talk about what you know, not what you don't.

The same goes for Monopoly. When you start losing, start focusing on what you can do instead of what you cannot. Do not assume you need to have something that you don't have in order to win. You can only move from the position of where you are, not from where you want to be.

Offend

Make someone look stupid in public and you have laid a land mine that will one day explode. Offend your boss and your days are numbered. There is no reward big enough to warrant this approach. Yes, you can prove that you are right, that you are a better player, but are you willing to lose the whole game? There are always other paths you can take.

Do not let your primeval brain control your need to show off or respond negatively in a heated argument. Once something is said, it is forever. Remember, this is Monopoly at work. It is not your family that will understand and accept you at all costs. They may accept you, but they don't have to play Monopoly with you. At work, offending another Monopoly player is indeed a risky move. It could cost you your job.

A Winning Strategy

In short, the rules of Monopoly center on winning, losing, relationships, and knowledge. They are not about effort, feelings, or problems. You either win or lose. You either have support or not. You provide information, have information, or are seeking information. Therefore, a winning strategy means to be in the know, build relationships, and create success. Nothing else matters in Monopoly, either at work or in the board game.

Success Behaviors

How do you implement a winning Monopoly strategy? The first thing is to never get lost in the weeds. Someone has to stay at the bridge and steer the ship. I have seen way too many leaders follow the path of fixing what they think are critical problems themselves and forgetting everything else. This always ends in disaster. Being in the know about one subject is not sufficient. As a leader, it is critical to decide what information is important to have when managing a group, so create a system where information flows easily to and from you. Build an information network with people who can help if additional support is needed. You cannot win if every disaster or problem requires a data-hunting expedition before any action can be taken. Therefore, being in the know is about building a system that can quickly provide the information you need.

The second thing to do is build a relationship with your manager, your peers, and your group. This takes time, and it requires constant attention. However, you cannot expect them to help you in a crisis or with a new opportunity if you do not have their support. Getting it is hard work. Ignoring it is failure. Asking for it only during a crisis is not a winning approach.

Lastly, show success widely and often. The more success you have now, the more you will have in the future. There is simply nothing better for success than success.

These approaches work well if you combine them with positioning yourself at the right place in the company. You cannot play Monopoly from home. You need a seat at the table. You get that by being in one or more of these place as listed below.

- Managing a large group.
- Owning a specific technology that is important for the company.
- Owning a flagship product.
- Owning a critical function, such as annual planning or budget reviews.
- Owning the budget, especially if other groups depend upon you.

Playing to Win

What does it mean to win at Monopoly? In the end, we can't all end up as the CEO. But we can keep playing, make a positive impact, get rewarded, and make the company more successful. However, all that is not enough for someone who is driven by gaining a title, and that will push them to play the game with only one purpose: win all the money and bankrupt every other player. But don't let that be you. Instead, look at playing Monopoly as a way of being the best you can be. As long as you can play, contribute, learn, grow, and be rewarded along the way, what more is needed? A title alone is never a measure of success.

Monopoly Forces at Work

Let's again return to the forces at work I described in chapter 1. These are the ones that occur as a direct result of Monopoly players' actions.

> **The annual reorganization:** *Your group has finally figured out how to get things done in an efficient manner. Then, all of a sudden, there is a reorganization. All the groups around you change names, and different leaders are appointed. Now you have to spend the next three months rebuilding your network and deciphering the best ways of getting things accomplished. Why?*

For some reason, this is the most common way leaders think a problem or system can be fixed: by reorganizing who reports to whom. In the process, they often forget or ignore that most people work across organizations and with people they know. Regardless, a reorganization happens when failure is felt at the senior leadership level or someone there achieves great success. Either way, the response is that something must be reorganized to address the problem or the new challenge. A reorganization is about failure (lack of control) or success (more control).

> **The new company-wide initiative:** *Executives brought in a consulting company to fix the slow-moving development process, and your project has been selected as the first one to be scrutinized—or, should I say, to benefit from these new ideas. You now have to spend the next three months hoping to survive the scrutiny. What is the best strategy, join or avoid?*

This is the storyteller at work. He or she was able to convince someone that his or her story is a great one. It came with a bold promise of a wonderful future with many riches. People with no or little understanding of a company's day-to-day workings descend upon it to make an impact by decree. It doesn't matter if it solves something or not. All that matters is that this initiative is implemented to ensure a successful ending to the story. Your opinion does not matter. Through time, many of these initiatives tend to fade out. And when they do, the storyteller fades as well, either by being given a different role or leaving the company.

> **The lack of executive support:** *Nothing seems to get done. It is impossible to stay focused on anything long enough to prove that it will work or not. As a result, your team is seeking a sponsor high up in the organization to help them remove roadblocks. They are looking for executive support making decisions in their favor or to have their back. But despite high hopes, nothing changes. In fact, the hope that the sponsor would make your life easier is shattered. What is wrong with your executives?*

When block or chess players approach the game of Monopoly, they do so as a guest. They are asking for help with their own games. And more often than not, they get support from the Monopoly player. It is easy to pledge aid: it costs nothing, and the executive hopes nothing will be required beyond that. Unless this request for support is going to help with their Monopoly performance, they will not take action. Their goals are driven by their own management layer, and as such will always take precedence. Therefore, you likely will not get much actionable support unless you bring with you a new opportunity for the Monopoly players. Hence, lead with an opportunity, follow with an ask.

Next Steps

At work you either play with blocks, chess or Monopoly. Which game do you play? Block players are the designers and builders of products and services. They are driven by innovation and the desire to be recognized as creators who solve customer problems. They work in teams to deliver value to customers. They are bound by rules that are driven by Dolphins, Aristotle, the Joker or Captain Nemo, each with its own pros and cons. Chess players are middle managers who try to outsmart one another to gain advantages for their team or themselves. They are navigating complicated social situations crowded by coworkers who have skills similar to that of the chess pieces themselves. Monopoly, the game of power is what drives the company leadership. Here you will find the most ruthless of players, and the riches of King Solomon. However, we don't always stay with one game forever. With more experience, we tend to seek out bigger challenges.

Eventually the time may come to move from one game to another. Perhaps taking the step into management, drive a new project, or taking on a senior leadership position. This joyous opportunity is typically followed by a struggle to establish oneself in a new role. Often not understanding why. Next, we will explore game transitions and why they are so challenging.

8

Game Transitions

Learning the rules and success behaviors of one game typically takes years. I have coached many people about the time and effort it takes, but it is always a tough pill to swallow. Sometimes ambition overshadows reality. The subtle nuances of the games are not obvious until one starts playing. On the surface they may look simple, but that is because of failure to understand and appreciate their complexities. It is time to remind ourselves of the four levels of competence.

- **Unconscious incompetence**: when a person does not understand or know how to do something and may not recognize his or her own incompetence.
- **Conscious incompetence**: when a person realizes he or she does not understand or know how to do something, but does realize the value of the knowledge and mastering the skill.
- **Conscious competence**: when a person knows how to do something, but has to concentrate intensely to execute the skill.
- **Unconscious competence**: when a person understands a subject and can perform the skill.

Once you have mastered a game, you can stay comfortable there for a long time, assuming the world around you doesn't change too much. The invisible rules you once could not see now assist you in making an impact. You are at a point where you don't have to spend time pushing against the rules. Instead, you work within the context of the rules and, therefore, achieve your idea of success.

Should you become bored or decide to move up in the organization into a more senior leadership role, the game changes. The complexity, the expanded network, the impact of failure, and the level of uncertainty are all different. It takes time to understand the new rules, especially when they are not written down. As such, this is when failure occurs and as a result, people lose their jobs. The reason this happens is twofold. One, the new game requires new behaviors, and second, the player is playing the game assuming rules from a different game. Because playing by these rules made him or her successful in the past, the player by default will keep applying the same approach.

Three things can now happen: you learn the rules, stay in the game, and keep advancing; you are promoted to a role where you hang on by doing just enough to avoid termination; or you fail and leave the company. This is where the saying "Promoted to their level of incompetence" is often used. In reality, this is not about competence per say, but rather unconscious incompetence. It is all about understanding and playing by a new set of rules, moving from conscious incompetence to unconscious competence.

Given sufficient motivation and determination, it is possible to become successful at the next level. However, many are not willing to make this investment. Accepting a new set of rules means starting from the bottom. It means giving up being in a lead role and moving into becoming part of the heard. You no longer stand out, you have to prove yourself all over again. Sadly, many get stuck in this transition. They see themselves through one lens only and are not willing to accept the changes a new game will require. But, I am going to assume that you are willing to cross over to a new game and tackle a new set of challenges. Why am I making this assumption? Simply because you are reading this book.

Preparing for a Game Transition

For the most part, a career will progress from playing with blocks to chess, and then perhaps move on to Monopoly. You have been working for a while and your skills and successes are noticed. And you are given an increase in responsibility and a bigger tile. Or you may seek out a better position that is located in a different game.

In some cases the starting game may be chess, having come from a management educational track. Starting at the chess level is different than moving from playing with blocks to chess. The biggest disadvantage is not being aware of block disasters that can easily be avoided. For example, I worked with one person who designed a change to the HR system by himself, sent me the one-pager for implementation and walked away. Expecting I would then easily be able to roll this out and collect the new data from every employee in the organization. Asking every block player in a larger organization to provide data is not a one-day job. On paper it seems simple, in reality it can take months to implement. In this case, the chess player should have assessed the effort required to implement versus the benefits, In addition, this project should also be compared to everything else that needed to be done. Simply moving forward solving every problem without an understanding of effort can result in low impact or failure.

Founders of successful start-ups grow with the company through these games. They have to start with a new idea or product. They have to show that their block-building skills can produce something great. As the company grows, more people join and chess games are forming. This is when founders start being uncomfortable, feeling the loss of control. As a result, they may have everyone report to them directly, or try to avoid any issue that looks like big-company politics. That can be discussing rules for salaries, vacation days, office locations, etc. As the company grows, someone has to spend time steering the ship. Setting goals, strategies, and ensuring that the collective efforts of all employees and partners are meeting revenue goals and shareholders expectations. This game is called Monopoly. This is when some founders throw in the towel and hire an experienced CEO or leadership team. While others, cling to the notion that they can build with blocks, avoid the chess game, and also be a star

Monopoly player. Many try this approach, but few can do it well. Do not try to play and control all games at once. Play the game you are in, but allow time for learning the next game. Once there, play that game. Leave the other game behind.

Regardless of your starting position, a successful transition requires preparation. First and foremost is accepting the existence of the three games. You don't have to be a master in all three before you start playing. You just have to know they are there. Your focus has to be on doing well in your current role, in your current game. Because that is the base where you can transition to another game. Second, seek out mentors, people who are already playing the game you want to join. They can provide insights about the rules. They may not use words like "games" and "rules," but they can show you what to do and what not to do. This is invaluable. And third, practice. You can start today by trying out some of the success behaviors that are required in the new game in your current game. This will give you an idea of what works for you and what areas you need to improve upon. You can also look for assignments or short-term projects that require frequent interaction with players of different games. For example, you may represent your group in an annual planning session with chess players, or you may represent a chess player at a budget-planning meeting with Monopoly players.

The more you practice, the better the chances for success in the next game. When you eventually make the move to a new game, reality will hit hard. Expectations are high, and time is limited. It is difficult to set aside time to determine the rules in the middle of a crisis. The more you can practice within the safety of your current game, the better.

Fuzzy Borders

A company may not always play games that fit neatly into the three clean categories. You often see people playing by different rules than others at the same level. That could be because they have not figured out the rules, or they are simply ignoring them. Or it can be that someone on the team is preparing for the next level and in the process are confusing other teammates about what is important and what success looks like.

For people playing with blocks, success means completing a task or shipping a product. For a person preparing for management, or chess, success is recognition. Sometimes they push into the limelight to gain an unfair advantage so they can elevate their position. In other cases, you may see a manager attend every meeting he or she can and ask big-picture questions, such as, "Why are we doing this?" or "Is there a better way?" These questions are meant to impress others and make them think that he or she is ready to play Monopoly, the game of power. In smaller organizations, you may experience all three games being played in the same set of cubicles. This type of game-mixing always creates confusion and unhappiness. I will talk more about this in the next chapter.

Erik N. Boe

9

Game Collisions

Moving from one game to another is a permanent, or a long-term event. It is a decision about a change in responsibilities. I call that a game transition. A game collision is a temporary event. Players from different games engage for a short time to address a particular issue or opportunity. It can happen at any time. It can be planned on unplanned.

Each level of a company plays a different game. It has its own set of rules. Building with blocks or bricks is about creativity and having fun. Chess is about logic and intelligence. Monopoly is about power and winning. As long as there is no interference, the players stick to the rules and play the game. However, once the games collide, things get interesting. For example, when an executive reaches down into the organization, connecting with a specific person for specific information, the cross-game dynamics focus on an exchange of intelligence and opportunity. The executive is seeking new opportunities to enable him or her to move ahead of the other players. At the same time, middle managers are searching for information that could place them in a better position as compared to other managers and groups.

Bad things happen when players are unaware that a collision is actually occurring. It may look like something isn't working and needs to be fixed, and if a fix is not possible, the typical result is finding someone or something to blame. Who failed to deliver? Who did not anticipate a particular question or need? The reality is that a fix is often not needed or even possible. You cannot change the fact that managing a company is different than developing a product. Each requires different skills and approaches. Someone skilled at one aspect will not necessarily be skilled at the other. When expert players of the same game compete, they can outplay one another in that game, but not when they join a different game. Therefore, what is needed is the awareness that another game is also being played.

Softening the Collision

In my early days at Apple when I was learning to play chess, I knew that the outcome would be uncertain if I approached executives with a new proposal or asked for money. So I approached such a game collision as I would have if I was making a movie. Just to be clear: I don't know how to make a movie, but I have seen many of them.

In short, I made sure that every meeting I had with executives was fully scripted and the outcome certain. Reaching that point took some preparation. First, I had to build a solid case. Then I approached every group that would have a representative at the executive meeting. I sought out the key leaders in each group who had the ear of the executives. I worked with them to make sure we were on the same page on the issue. I did not approach them with a solution, but rather with a common problem. From there we worked together to outline a solution. I then made sure that my original ask was part of that solution and was incorporated into the proposal. If needed, I also individually met with executives well before the meeting or asked my executive sponsor to reach out to them. By the time the meeting occurred, it was a simple matter of presenting the facts and sitting back to await the secured outcome.

Not every situation warranted this preparation, but if it was important, it was the path I chose. I made it my preferred approach when visiting the game of Monopoly. I wanted no surprises. I had seen just too many failures.

Collisions Are Directional

There are three games that can collide. That is a total of three types of collisions. But the collisions are directional, leading to a total of six different situations. Yes, there is one more kind of collision. That is when all three games collide.

As long as you remain within the borders of your own game, you can play using established rules. However, when you cross game borders, things change. When a manager connects with executives, cross-game dynamics come into play. The same holds true when a project team reaches out to their manager.

When someone joins a Monopoly game, the currency for those players is a new opportunity. This could mean a possibility to gain an advantage, such as the ability to buy more properties or passing start to collect $200.

Chess players seek intelligence, something that can reveal the opponent's weaker side or give them a leg up. They are not looking for advice, but rather information that they can themselves interpret and use for their next moves.

Interestingly enough, people playing with blocks are also looking for new opportunities, but not to win over others. Instead, they want more blocks or opportunities to build something new, bigger, or better. Anything that results in more blocks is better. With this in mind, let's take a look at what happens when the games collide.

When Building with Blocks Collides with Chess

As part of everyday work, it is normal that team members contact their managers when they need help, guidance, or money. Their motive is to make sure they provide the best possible product or service.

When an engineer reaches out to the management team and asks for more people, he or she needs to know that chess players want bigger benefits than just meets the eye. They are asking themselves questions like,

"What would be better for the group after the resources are added?" or "How will this move the group and the management into a better light as compared with other groups?" In some cases, it may be simple to see that adding people will make a big difference. In other cases, no external benefit can be shown. The ask should not focus only on fixing team problems or design challenges. It needs to include visible benefits for chess players. Anything that lacks benefits but promises to resolve internal team turmoil can easily be ignored.

When managers reach out to their teams, it is to obtain status, set directions, or resolve team conflicts. In some situations, managers think they are part of the block-building team and become involved in the construction. But at the point when they are playing with blocks, they have abandoned the chess game. This should be a warning signal for the team, as it now has managers paying little attention to the group's overall direction. Left unchecked, this will in no time negatively impact the group.

If a manager reaches out to a team, it is not really to hear about why things are not working. They are there to obtain success stories and showcase them. They are looking for improvements, ideas, or new directions. In the absence of success, managers get involved to help the group. That could mean moving people from one team to another, promoting employees who have demonstrated a new level of success, or changing workflow processes. A successful manger wants his or her team to be successful. That shows great leadership skills.

When Building with Blocks Collides with Monopoly

On occasion, a block-building team members reach out to executives, the Monopoly players. This could be driven by a lack of clarity offered at the management level, the chess players. A team member may feel compelled to get to the bottom of a situation by finding clear directions. Sometimes this works. But in most cases, the Monopoly players themselves are not organized, nor that closely aligned, that a simple answer is available. If there is an explicit ask for change, that is typically handed back to the chess players to implement. Monopoly players do not play with blocks or chess.

They know that promising changes will not happen unless changes are made within the chess and block-building groups.

The exception is if a person building with blocks has already shown that he or she can drive the delivery of a new product or a solution that will make a major difference for the company. In those cases, the Monopoly players will listen, because they are comfortable with such moves. In other words, you do something big for me, and I will repay the favor. Block-building team members who can pull this off are rare, but they can be found. In those rare occasions, their peers respect them for their accomplishments and their ability to gain the ear of executives. At the same time, they are often envied by chess players.

It is unusual that Monopoly players directly reach out to block-building team members. This is normally done through chess players, in which case the chess players control the interaction. If they do reach out, it is to someone they already know, and to someone who has a track record of solving challenging problems that Monopoly players care about. Such as adding a great feature to their flagship product. The reason for the outreach can be to gain insight into a problem that the chess players have not managed very well. In short, the executives are seeking to understand, gain insight, and therefore leverage.

When Chess Collides with Monopoly

Many chess players are drawn to Monopoly, but some are not. They can see the toll it can take on a person. These people instinctively know that it is a different game. They may not know the rules, but they do understand that it requires much effort. So they avoid it, participating only when necessary. Hence, they may not spend time preparing for theses collisions. This is always a mistake. as these collisions happen frequently.

When a chess player who wants to play Monopoly approaches the Monopoly game, it is often to gain recognition and, in the process, be seen as a person who can create value. Monopoly recognition gives them an advantage in chess. So when a chess player visits a Monopoly game, it is important that he or she does not present problems or opportunities that are solely based upon a logic.

For example, do not make a million-dollar ask for a new test facility simply because current testing procedures are inadequate. Even the best argument will fall to the wayside if the Monopoly player does not believe in testing quality in the product in the first place (as compared to writing great code in the first place). When Steve Jobs came back to Apple in 1997, a five-hundred-person quality/test organization was reduced to five people. He simply did not believe that a central group could improve product quality. Therefore, a chess player approaching Monopoly must test the waters rather than rely solely upon a logical approach that concludes that product quality will improve by adding more people.

Monopoly players use chess players to give them more power, drive results, and solve big business challenges. This is typically measured in revenue growth, margins, customer satisfaction, and product quality. Their interaction tends to be focused on reaching goals and obtaining success. This is how Microsoft PowerPoint and Excel have come to dominate the communication channels in corporate America. Both are simple to customize, and neither are connected to the real world or to databases, therefore enabling chess players to "interpret" the state of the business for the Monopoly players. This is a perfect place for chess players. They use slides and spreadsheets to control their own destinies and in the process, obtain recognition from Monopoly players.

When Three Games Collide

This happens for the most part in very specific circumstances. For example, a company meeting with one-way communication. A tiger team is created to solve a very specific problem. Or, you work in a small start-up. The difference in these cases as compared to two-game collisions is that you immediately recognize these three-game collisions. They are often very tense and hence, capture our attention. They all signal that something special is taking place.

In a company meeting an employee asked the CEO a challenging question. Next to me, a senior manager said to another senior manager "I am glad he is not reporting to me!" The inference was that this question would have consequences across all three games. First up to the Monopoly players, then down to the chess players, who then would trickle down any fall-out to employees playing with blocks.

A tiger team may be created and asked to traverse across all teams and games. I have seen this work well. I have also seen total failure. It all depend upon the tiger teams awareness and skills of the topics outlined in this book.

A start-up offers a close-up to all three games at once. You may walk from an engineering meeting into a board presentation about market share. In the hall-way into the meeting you may talk to other managers about next month's key goals. This can be invigorating. It can also be taxing. In either case, it offers opportunities for rapid learnings.

Translators

How can a company function when three different games are being played simultaneously? How do they work well together? How do things get done? And who can keep track of it all?

Sometimes it seems like a miracle that an organization can deliver anything of value. Sometimes things simply do not get done. Improper flow of information among games may prevent the company from doing the right things. This can happen when a company grows rapidly. It takes time for players to settle into the games and establish communication channels. During these times, it is difficult to form connections between games. It can also happen when a company runs into financial troubles. You then have Monopoly players downsizing chess and block-building employees, and as a result, chaos ensures.

Efficient communication flow is critical. You cannot afford to have executives make plans and then forget to inform the chess players, who then in turn ask the block-building teams to build the wrong things. Companies that do well have translators. These are employees who translate information among the games. Sometimes they have a senior title, such as chief of staff, vice president of operations, program manager, director, or product lead. But for the most part, they do not have an impressive title. They fall into these roles after acquiring the translation skill through experience and a lot of hard work. These employees are invaluable. They help groups and individuals obtain needed support. This is a critical aspect of running a successful organization.

For example, say you were to ask your management for additional people for a project you are running. You normally aren't awarded more people unless you have a good case. How well you present that case is dependent upon how well you prepare to answer the questions the decision-makers will likely ask. The translators will know. They will help you make concise and convincing proposals, successfully translating a block-building request into a chess ask.

Successful translators can be found anywhere in the leadership branch. The better they are at translating, the better their own groups will respond. For instance, how would you translate executive goals, such as growing market share or revenue? A project team cannot deliver revenue growth since they develop products. Ten percent revenue growth, year over year, is meaningful to Monopoly players, but not to block-building teams. For them, this goal does not invoke a sense of purpose. Instead, they must be inspired and enabled to deliver a product that will make a difference. A translator will interpret goals into something a project team can believe in. Translators are the invisible enablers of company success. For the most part, what they do is not appreciated enough. Should you know one, be sure to make them part of your inner circle. They make things happen.

Having said this, there are of course many senior leaders and managers who are great at translating company vision into motivating team goals. However, very often not enough time or effort is spent keeping this connection alive. It is not enough to define yearly or even quarterly goals. One has to make sure that this connection is kept up and fine-tuned every day. And in the whirlwind of every-day work, this focus is often lost.

There are of course CEO's and senior leaders who can connect with employees at all levels. And those people do make a difference. But that is not the same as being there and supporting employees with everyday challenges. Only translators across the company can fill that role.

The Games Form One System

Regardless of the primary game you play, you have to be aware of the others that are taking place around you. You don't have to be skilled in all of them, but you do need to know how they can impact you. If you ignore them, you will be surprised sooner rather than later. You may do everything right, but one day you will find that your project is canceled. And that is a surprise you do not want to experience.

When playing your game, spend time keeping up with events in the other games. It will give you tremendous insight into what is really happening at the company. Set up meetings with people from all the games. If you are a manager in a chess game, become a mentor or sponsor for block-building team members. Seek mentors from the Monopoly game. It is important that this outreach be about learning and mutual exchange of information, not about a particular problem or challenge. It needs to be done at a personal level, where company interests are temporarily set aside. Yes, it is time-consuming and may not be very exciting. But you will build direct communication channels across all three games. That is something that will be incredible beneficial, regardless of the game you are playing.

Erik N. Boe

10

Managing the Games

At this point, you may wonder if a better approach to individual and company success is to abolish the idea of these games altogether. Or you may think that the impact of these games is minimal and can be ignored. My take on this is that as long we as are dealing with people and organizations, these dynamics will remain. Remove the organization and you have different dynamics. Remove people and then dynamics can be ignored. We all have ideals we strive for, priorities we support. It is easy to envision solutions that everyone should implement. But, we live in a complex society. The reality of the world is not playing out according to one person's ideas, but rather according to the accumulated set of likes and dislikes of people across the planet. In short, our collective behaviors are cemented by human interactions.

Influencing the Rules

The best way to manage a company and influence the games is to establish a company identity. An organization needs to know what it stands for and what it is striving to become. Something must drive the everyday efforts of every employee. A company purpose must be understood and fully embraced. Leaders across the company must be encouraged to live up to this purpose; no exceptions can be afforded. Just like when you teach your children to cross the street, there is never any situation when you avoid using the crosswalk. One exception will open the door to using the crosswalk only when convenient. As humans, we are incredibly good at justifying our reasoning and actions. Therefore, always use the crosswalk. No exceptions.

It is critical to establish a company way of being. That way can be anything you like. There is no right or wrong approach. Either you have one or you don't. When designing your organization, here are some important questions. What will drive your innovation pipeline? What are the results you want? Who will be part of the company? How will success be measured? Or, put in another way: how are you going to create value?

Once this is clear, use your approach across the whole company to model which rules are important in each game. For example, if being honest is critical during product development, then no exceptions are allowed. Holding back bad news about a future ship date cannot be tolerated. At the same time, being the bearer of bad news cannot be punished.

If collaboration is critical at the management layer, then reward managers reaching joint goals across groups. Hold executives accountable for really connecting with chess players to ensure that plans are not made in a vacuum and for creating goals that inspire block-builders.

It is not possible to eliminate the games, but it is possible to influence their rules at the macro level. As a company, the goal should be to emphasize what is important and what is not. Then, live that every day.

Connecting the Games

How does a company become successful? The answer: when each game is allowed to operate to serve its purpose. That is, block players produce value, chess players create plans that allocate resources to high-priority goals, and the Monopoly players steer the company into the right markets and ensure protection from competition and external threats. In addition, there is one more critical step. Keep the games connected. In my experience, the lack of game connections is what makes or breaks a company. You can have the best engineers in the world working on the best technology, but wrong timing and wrong market could kill the company. Even the best leaders will fail if they cannot connect with chess players who direct the majority of the employees. Unfortunately, these connections are often overlooked in larger companies. The prevailing assumption is that once the Monopoly players understand what needs to be done, the rest is "elementary."

When you have a large number of people working toward what is called a common goal, it is easy to find confusion, misinformation, or even opposing goals. As humans, we are easily distracted. We interpret the world very differently than our coworkers. Remember the game of telephone? In a row of say six to seven people, the first person whispers a sentence to the person by his or her side. Then this person whispers the "same" sentence to the person next to him or her. Finally, the last person speaks out loudly what he or she heard. Then the first person shares what he or she initially communicated. What you will find is most certainly a big difference. This is how companies work. Communication trickles down from executives via multiple levels of managers. When it reaches the block players, the original meaning is lost.

Maintaining the integrity of company goals, strategy, and direction is more challenging than creating them in the first place. This is why companies struggle. We are all smart, educated, and know how to get things done. Why is alignment around simple messages so difficult? The short answer is that we are human. As this book explains, different motives and views of the world leads to different interpretation of information, which again leads to different behaviors.

The Founder's Trap

I have already mentioned how founders of a company can have trouble growing their company. I call this the founder's trap. Believing that the road to success is to compress all games into one. Initially, a founder is successful because he or she is able to create a great block structure. As the company grows, the founder needs to leave that behind and start playing chess. This is where the founder starts feeling the loss of control. Some can make that transition while others cannot. Either way, it is a tough learning experience. If the company goes public, the founder is now forced to start playing Monopoly. Some fumble, the company dies, or the founder leaves. Others learn to work through it. These transitions are tough. Founders have withdrawal symptoms and are under the illusion that they can play all three games at once. Maybe they can, but not for long. At some point, something will break. Successful founders are quick learners and will use this failure as a stepping stone to future success. Others clamp down and the company is forever trapped by itself. The founder's trap is to believe that they can "will" the world to work for them. They are not willing to accept that a company that grows needs to allow for the formation of the three games.

Maintaining the Rules

It is simply not possible to remove a game. As long as there are groups of people formed to achieve a common purpose, these games will prevail. It is also impossible to remove rules from a game. The best you can hope for is that the players are following some rules more than others. And those rules should be aligned with the company's reason for being.

Most companies have an established set of rules for specific actions, such as taking time off, submitting expense reports, and so on. One universal order that should be implemented is that all those rules should be followed. Allowing anarchy is not a good idea, so enforce the rule that employees are expected to follow company guidelines. This means that if you know of rules that don't make sense, change or remove them—but do not break them.

Translators

Use translators as much as possible. They understand how to make things happen. They have the wisdom and insight into resolving conflicts and enabling people to contribute at their fullest potential. They are also the guards against reorganizations to fix perceived block-building problems. Monopoly players do not build with blocks and should not routinely move these teams around in the hope of producing better Monopoly results. It is simply too costly and can take a better part of a year before a large organization recovers from a substantial reorganization. An annual reorganization and reduction in the workforce dramatically reduces the company's chances of success.

Translators also provide guidance on what company-wide initiatives are worth implementing. Most are not. Only if they truly become part of everyone's tasks will they stick—in other words, if they create habits. That will happen only when the interest comes from all participants in the games. One game cannot make other games change without every impacted employee's full support.

Achieving Success

In short, companies are successful when they realize that three games are being played simultaneously. They accept it and endeavor to have players follow positive rules rather than destructive ones. They also see the critical need for translators to ensure that each game is played with minimal interruption by other games. The more experienced translators a company has, the better the chances of success. Now, let's move on to the last chapter of the book—a summary of all the key concepts. If you decide to do anything, print these pages and staple them to the wall. It will give you a quick synopsis of playing with blocks, chess, and Monopoly at work.

Erik N. Boe

11

The Games in a Nutshell

By now, you may have many questions about the concepts you have read about in this book. So, how should you proceed from here? Well, it depends upon your situation and motives. I will assume you read this book to learn more about corporate America and how to become successful. Therefore, I will use this last chapter to summarize the book's main points and point out what to do next. This will propel you forward on your journey of making you and your organization more successful.

The Games

A large organization is a chaotic place filled with events and situations that can seem unexplainable. Revealing the invisible forces at work will clarify why things happen. The forces become visible by understanding the rules that govern corporate America. The great thing about these rules is that you can use them to better predict future outcomes, thereby making it possible to create a winning approach at any level of the organization.

Understanding the invisible forces at work is done by applying the perspectives of block-builders, chess, and Monopoly players. Block-building is where the value for customers is created. This is where new ideas are formed, implemented, delivered, and supported. This game is about creativity. Block-builders are the product development teams and people on the front line. Chess is the infrastructure that holds the organization together. This is where policies and initiatives are defined, and planning occurs. This game is about logic and reason. Chess players are middle management and senior leaders. Executives of the company play Monopoly. This game is about power, resources, money, and big titles. It is about winning at all costs.

The Players

First we have the block-builders. They fall into four groups described as Dolphins, Aristotle, Captain Nemo, and the Joker. The Dolphins are neither destructive nor harmful, but they are focused on themselves as the center of the universe. An Aristotle group has less emotions and looks at the world logically. And if everyone did that, there should be less conflict and crisis, hence everyone should get along. On the contrary, a Captain Nemo group distances itself from the larger organization and creates its own superior team, absolved from any rules but their own. Finally, we have the Joker group, which is out to change the dysfunctional world and in the process creates crisis after crisis.

Chess is about envisioning the future and predicting the most likely outcome. But at its core, it is about understanding one's opponent. Many of the opponents can be described by chess pieces. The king is someone who makes the final decisions. The queen stays close to the king and often strikes out to enforce his directives. Rooks rely on brute power. Bishops are good at circumventing the most common obstacles. Knights are fearless and often push boundaries. The pawns are focused on doing their job, and seek to avoid conflicts and changes. Each type of player demands a different approach when being engaged.

Monopoly is about power. The rules are very simple, and they have been part of history for millennia. They are best envisioned by thinking about medieval Europe, with constant wars among rulers hiding behind castle walls.

The Rules

There are two sets of rules when playing with blocks. The first is to accept and abide by all legal and company policies and accepted social behavior. The second set is derived from the group itself. This set is divided into four categories covering the range of social behavior.

For the Dolphins the rules are: We must all prove ourselves, so take no prisoners; building is done primarily to show that we know how to solve tough problems. We are the only ones who truly know how to build something; we know what we are doing, so we build big and only test in production; we don't have to ask for input. Building is all about having fun; we are great—so build anything. Sorry, I cannot help you, as I am busy rebuilding what broke yesterday. There are only a few people in our group who can decide how to build something; everyone else must follow their lead. We build separately and hopefully never have to combine what we build into one thing. We will never stop adding blocks to our structure, regardless of how big it gets, because this is a great work of art.

Aristotle rules are: A project follows a very well-defined process where information is made widely available; there is very little outside interference, as everybody knows who is in charge and how decisions are made. We build as a team. A product can ship only when every criteria is met. No exceptions. Everyone is allowed to fill their role as best as they can; very little bickering among employees is tolerated. The focus is on customer problems and reasonable solutions, within given time and cost parameters. There are clear rules for how a team is awarded. There is a common understanding of why the team exists and how it relates to other teams; each team may have different goals, which is OK, but collectively, they all support the bigger goal. Building is about solving customer problems, so let's at least talk to some of them.

Captain Nemo's rules are: Through suffering, we arrived at a view of the world that will allow us to create technologies and solutions far beyond anybody else's capabilities. We don't owe anybody anything. We are capable of doing whatever we want rules are for everyone else; our own abilities will not be restricted by following the larger group's methodologies. Build small, then validate; learn; then build bigger; how big can we build? The best product wins; everyone is encouraged to experiment with any type of blocks or bricks and build any structure. Do not touch our blocks!

And the final set of block-building rules come from the Joker: Ship on time; regardless of what is built, it must ship on time; it doesn't matter if anybody wants it or if it works; it just needs to ship on time; I will not tell you what to build, but I expect it to be delivered on time. Change will happen, so get used to it. Every day is a new challenge; expect a constant string of changes and surprises every day you go to work. Planning ahead is not important, as plans will change; instead, we will react quickly when change happens. Build the product and show me; then I will decide if it is good. We will never be given enough time or resources to do what we want, so we have to step up our efforts. New challenges bring out the best in people and will show others what we are made of.

The chess rules can be summarized in one word—know your opponents. This will guide you in how to work with and how to best approach them. This game being about logic, the additional rule is to plan ahead for your next moves. Chess players tend to be predictable in their behaviors as they have applied them often to get where they are today. And they are very reluctant to change. Their behaviors can be described by the chess pieces themselves: The king makes decisions. The queen moves fast and far and has power to change almost everything. Rooks moves in straight lines and once in motion does not stop easily. The bishop moves in unpredictable paths and has surprising ideas. The knights are fearless attackers that often seek out conflicts; pawns just want to do their jobs.

In the present day, Monopoly rules are as follows: The person with the biggest title calls the shots. Leaders of flagship products get the first pick. A storyteller is given the chance to implement his or her ideas. Success opens doors, and failure closes them. Employee support matters, as does proximity to the CEO. Inability to defend your position leads to failure. Offending other players will eliminate you from the game.

Currency

Block-builders are seeking opportunities to build something new, bigger, or better. Chess players want intelligence, something that can reveal information about opponents and give them a leg up. The currency for Monopoly players is a new opportunity, a possibility to gain an advantage that leads to a better position in the game.

Winning

Triumphing at block-building is the ability to continue creating something new as long as you want in any role you desire. The success behavior is to create win-win scenarios whenever you can and establish and maintain good personal relationships at work.

Winning at chess is retaining the ability to keep playing the game, while advancing both your group and your career at the same time without harming others. The success behavior is to demonstrate real success often and broadly, align all your goals with key company goals, and have executive support behind all your important projects.

To win at Monopoly is to stay in the game, have a positive impact, gain rewards, and make the company successful. The success behavior is to be in the know, invest in building relationships with your managers and peers, and demonstrate success widely and often.

Transitions

A successful transition requires preparation. First and foremost is accepting the existence of the three games. Second, seek out mentors, people who are already playing the game you want to join. And third, practice. You can start today by trying out some of the success behaviors that are required in the new game in your current game.

Collisions

Employees who are part of one game will often interact with employees from other games. The edges of the games are fuzzy. It may not be clear what rules are most important to follow or what approach to take. But the important thing is to recognize when collisions are occurring and move carefully.

Block-builders and chess players interact frequently. Block-builders reach out for help with a problem or to better understand directions and limitations. Chess players reach out primarily to learn about successes, obtain status, set direction, or to resolve team problems.

On occasion, block-builders reach out to Monopoly players. This is often caused by chess players not providing enough information. Monopoly players reach out to block-builders to get clarity for the same reason, namely confusion created by or inaction on the part of the chess players.

Chess players reach out to Monopoly players to gain recognition, show their value, and get an advantage in their own chess game. Monopoly players reach out to chess players to drive results and solve business challenges.

There are times when all three games collide. Typically in situations such as company meetings or when tiger teams are formed to address specific problems. You often see three-game collisions in start-ups.

Companies that do well have translators. For the most part, they do not have a senior title. These are employees who translate information between the games, information that makes it possible for everyone to know what needs to get done and why. The biggest part of this role is to provide appropriate motivation for all groups, which is often done by reinterpreting goals or challenges given to them by players in other games.

Managing the Games

The best way to manage a company and influence the games is to establish a company identity. An organization needs to know what it stands for and what it is striving to become. Something must drive the everyday efforts of every employee. It is not possible to eliminate the games, but it is possible to influence their rules at the macro level. As a company, the approach to manage the games is be to emphasize what is important and what is not. Then, live that every day.

Successful companies allow each game to operate to serve its purpose. That is, block players produce value, chess players create plans that allocate resources to high-priority goals, and the Monopoly players steer the company into the right markets and ensure protection from competition and external threats. In addition, there is one more critical step. Keep the games connected. The best way is to leverage translators who can guide players toward common goals, articulated in ways all players can understand. The lack of connected games lead to company failure.

Next

As you start taking the next step on your career ladder, do so by following an approach that lets you quickly learn and improve. There is simply no way of entering these games with all the answers at hand, so the best approach is to be prepared to learn. The quicker you learn, the faster you can move ahead. The approach to getting started at any level of this ladder is fairly simple: Observe, Play, Reflect, Repeat.

Step one is to go to work and look around. Determine what game is being played. Label the players. Look for their motivations. Predict the future. Sit back and wait. Did your prediction come true? If not, try again. You are now on your way to becoming a winner. This state of the learning process is risk free. You don't have to do anything differently. All you have to do is look at your surroundings from the perspective of the games. They bring new colors, patterns, and eventually an understanding of corporate America. And that is great. It is like discovering a hidden dimension to life.

Step two is to play. Put plans into action. What you are doing is seeing how the players will react to your moves. They are not reacting to ideas you read in a book. This is now all about your actions. You are the one who has to learn how your moves will work for or against you based upon what you can do. You have to establish yourself in the game before you can win.

Step three is to take a mental break and reflect on how the game is going for you. Did a certain approach work well? Was that success an accident or can it be repeated? Can you leverage some of your learnings in other areas? As you learn more ways of playing the game, your approach will become refined and less error prone. Over time, you will establish a method that will work for you.

Step four is to return to step one. Observe the organization with your new learnings in mind. But this time, tackle bigger challenges. If you don't find them, create them. You may have to start small. For example, if you want to take on more responsibilities, you can do something like creating a group blog to showcase the groups success. Observe how this project is recognized. If it is appreciated and makes an impact, move on to a higher-risk project to further your success in the game.

I Wish You Success!

And that it is. This last chapter summarized the key ideas in this book and is the base for which to engage successfully with corporate America. It is a place like everywhere else—driven by human needs and desires. It has been studied and documented in depth for a long time. It may have its challenges, but it also offers a world of wonderful opportunities, so embrace it. Make the best of it. Never take what happens to you personally. Your value as a person is not at stake in the corporate games. What *is* at stake is your ability to participate and be successful. Therefore, use the ideas in this book to become a better player, a more valuable employee. Take advantage of learning every day. Move forward by taking small steps. Your ability to learn and the desire to be successful is what really matters. I wish you success!

Play

Erik N. Boe

About the Author

Born in Norway, Erik N. Boe moved in 1986 to California to join the personal computer revolution. He earned a bachelor's degree in computer science from the University of California, Santa Barbara, followed by a master's in international business from Pepperdine University in Southern California.

Erik started his career with Apple in 1991. He was there before, during, and after the company's turnaround, first in the Mac OS group and later in the hardware division. He held positions ranging from software engineer, manager, and program manager; driving company-wide efforts focused on optimizing technology delivery and innovation. He has also worked for Adobe, where he was part of a global technology group delivering software components to all Adobe product teams. This central and unique position enabled him to gain deep insight into product development and innovation across the company.

Erik currently works at VMware, defining and implementing portfolio management and software delivery models. He lives in California with his wife, three children, a dog, and cat.

www.ingramcontent.com/pod-product-compliance
Lightning Source LLC
Chambersburg PA
CBHW070045210526
45170CB00012B/591